TALES OF BIG JON AND OTHER CREATURES

The Extraordinary Times of an Ordinary Family

ALLAN M. ARMITAGE

ISBN 9781088004982 (print)

ISBN 9781088005064 (ebook)

Library of Congress Control Number: 2021920322

Praise for
Tales of Big Jon and Other Creatures

"As the father of three grown sons and grandfather to two grandsons, I ended up reading the book twice because I was so entertained by the trials and tribulations of raising a family. Life is truly the most unscripted thing any of us will ever experience and Allan and Susan's journey together moved my emotions as I thought about my own family. Well done, Allan!"

—Steve Argo, father of three, grandfather of two

"Allan has a wonderful knack for storytelling. This book is so relatable to everyone. The family confessions of this ordinary family will keep you laughing, reminiscing, and entertained from beginning to end. A great weekend read! Enjoy!"

—Kitty Lay, mother of Rusty and Chip

"Raising children is frustrating, fun, worrisome and rewarding. Always a great storyteller, Armitage shares laugh-out-loud tales of raising his three kids. Veteran parents will recognize aspects of many of these stories, and newer parents will know they aren't alone."

—Robin Siktberg, mother of Eric and Lauren

"As a writer and a Mom, I so enjoyed *Tales of Big Jon and Other Creatures*. In a world where parenting seems sometimes an effort to avoid the swamp monsters of excess, sloth, and irresponsibility which want to eat our kids and our hearts as well, it's a joy and a comfort to settle back and sink into stories that make you smile. Armitage's own very personal reminiscences will help you remember your parenting victories and defeats and give you a space to retreat from the perils out there."

—Pamela Jekel, bestselling author of *Seastar*, *Columbia*, *Bayou*, and *The Third Jungle Book*

"This book is absolutely hilarious! Each tale resonated my own experiences with my children and I found myself literally laughing out loud. Each story left me anticipating the next, I wanted to read more. Even if you don't have children, this book brings back your childhood memories and is a wonderfully relatable book for everyone."

—Karen Ponder, mother of three super kiddos
and hoping for grandchildren—soon

"I was delighted each time this storytelling grandfather enchanted and entertained his grandchildren with antics and adventures of their parents' childhoods. A wonderful read."

—Sandi MacKenzie, mother of two
and grandmother of three

"Allan Armitage has always been famous for flowers and gardens but not known as a humorist! He has now excelled in one of the most heart-warming and funny books that I have had the pleasure of reading in a long time. We had four children and thought that no one could beat our stories, Allan has done it! These tales of funny family foolishness will bring chuckles, smiles, and tender memories of your family and your times with young children! A great read to forget your cares and just laugh."

—Barbara Dooley, mother of four,
grandmother of eleven

"As I read these wonderful stories, I recalled the memorable years of parenthood. And the reasons why I took up gardening. Alone. Outside."

—Lis Friemoth, mother of three,
grandmother of four

My childhood memories with four sisters and the antics of my three children (one with Down Syndrome) were brought to mind as I read this book. I laughed, I (happy) cried and I reminisced as I shared in the journey of the Armitage family.

—Joan Baird, mother of three,
grandmother of one
(hoping for more)

Dedication

To my family: Luck has little to do with success. Most people would say that hard work, commitment and persistence are far more important. However, as this book shows, family is the key to many of life's successes, and I have been blessed. As you turn the pages and meet my family, you will quickly agree. Sharing their adventures and misadventures (with their permission) as they evolved from children, to young adults, to parents raising children of their own, has been an immense pleasure. Thank you all.

• • •

To Extra Special People: Susan and I have been fortunate to know remarkable parents like Joan and Robert Baird and their wonderful child, Hannah. We have watched as they, among many others, focused their passion and love for children with disabilities through an amazing and special organization called *Extra Special People* (ESP). Susan and I have been stunned by the support of the communities and people who believe in ESP (espyouandme.org*)*.

ESP exists to create transformative experiences for people of all disabilities and their families, changing communities for the better. Based in Athens, Georgia, ESP offers summer camp and daily enrichment programs; family support such as retreats, dinners, and counseling; a mobile coffee cart, Java Joy, that employs adults with disabilities; and Camp Hooray, a 90-acre property with an aim to be the country's first universally accessible camp, retreat center, and much more. ESP welcomes over 700 families and participants from across the Southeast, all with a variety of diagnoses such as Cerebral Palsy, Down syndrome, Autism, Traumatic Brain Injury, Spina Bifida, and more. Participants and families are never turned away from ESP because of their ability or finances.

Unfortunately, passion, dedication, and love can only do so much to help children with disabilities. It costs $250,000 to raise a typical child; however, it costs $2.5 million to raise a child with a disability. Funding is essential for people with disabilities to have access to typical experiences.

I feel honored to be able to dedicate a percentage of all sales from this book to ESP. I hope we can all make a difference.

At ESP's summer camp, campers can receive "brags," a special recognition to celebrate their accomplishments. Sydney received a brag, shared by her friends, for having the most joyful smile around! Wouldn't you agree?

Hannah Baird and Allan Armitage, as always sharing a smile

Contents

Acknowledgments

"No matter what accomplishments you make, somebody helped you."

—Althea Gibson

So many people have been involved in this small book. How do I thank my incredibly long-suffering wife and my equally tolerant children as they rolled their eyes at me every time I asked "Do you remember the time . . . ?" They really were very normal children, they simply gave me so much good material to work with.

Valarie Nichols. Her illustrations have made these rather delightful stories even more delightful. In fact, I would not have ever written this book if I was unable to find such a passionate and talented person. Thank you.

Kirsten Dennison. Kirsten has the patience of Job. Her experience in layout and editing made my very rough document actually look like a book. Her talent has resulted in a clean and comfortable read.

Polly Brennan. Polly is a wordsmith. She took my poor punctuation, my dozens of misspellings, my many nonsensical paragraphs and numerous other literary blunders, and patiently corrected them all.

WHAT IS PAST IS PROLOGUE

It was a lovely day to do a little shopping in Augusta, Georgia. My wife, Susan, and I were checking out furnishings at a local shop. Elsewhere, our daughter Heather was running errands with her ten-year-old twins, Ben and Will. Then my wife's phone rang.

Suddenly my daughter screamed and the phone went silent.

After yelling her name a half-dozen times into the dead phone, we looked at each other, leapt into the car, and raced towards her home. All manner of horror filled our heads: car crash, mugging, children on the side of the road, ambulances . . .

We pulled into her driveway just a few minutes after Heather arrived. There she was, standing outside the car, soaking wet with bedraggled hair and dripping clothes. She glared at me with nary a smile on her lips and said, "Dad, how old do they have to be before I can kill them?"

It turns out that as she was taking the car through the car wash, and chatting with her mother, the twins reached up and pushed the button to open the sunroof. Before she could do anything, a torrent of soapy water had enveloped them. They made the drive home awash in water, suds, and puddles—Heather cussing in the front seat and the twins cowering in the back, as far from their mother as possible.

When we arrived, the twins had already disappeared, and as angry as our daughter was, we were doing everything we could not to start laughing. But when the dog walked up to us, shaking off the soapy residue and not at all happy, we lost it. Not exactly the supportive parents Heather was hoping for, but oh my, what a scene.

• • •

Welcome to the chaos and joy that family brings over the years. The stories I'm sharing are likely little different than those of your families, only the names are different.

It all started many years ago when I was lying on a couch . . .

Yo, Joe!

I recall it well. Many years ago, I had a very sore and swollen left knee, not from a sporting injury or a mismanaged fall, but rather the result of a karate chop professionally delivered by a four-year-old G.I. Joe. I was minding my own business when I heard a blood-curdling "Yo, Joe!" Jonathan, our youngest, also known as "Big Jon," twirled deftly on one foot and delivered the fatal blow with the other. As I recoiled in pain, I wondered if G.I. Joe had a father. I bet he limped a lot.

Such are my thoughts as I record stories many parents have experienced. To be a parent, grandparent, or godparent is to have memories of the crazy things our children do. When the kids are young, we laugh about these antics to friends and family, but as we get older those stories, as memorable as they were, fade with time. I too have put on a few years and my memory is not particularly sharp, but unlike many parents, I wrote the stories down.

I don't suppose that tales of this family are a great deal different than those echoing around any family, yet I hope that as you read them, those once-memorable adventures with your children will come alive again.

Come join me, Big Jon, and his sisters through some of our more unforgettable moments—some hilarious, some happy, and some sad. One thing I can assure you: I could not possibly make these up.

LAURA

"No, I won't do it." With these words, she flung off her wedding dress and tossed it on top of her already rejected veil. She loved the dress, but when she tried it on, it was at least six inches too short, to say nothing of the hideous veil that soared a good eight inches above her head. When Susan suggested she could sew a new section to increase the length of the gown, Laura rebelled. "I have been wearing ruffles to make my clothes longer my entire life—I am not going to wear ruffles on my wedding day!"

Of course, she had a point. Laura had been taller than all her friends and classmates since she was born, and getting pants to reach below her ankles or blouses to fit had always been exercises in making do.

After all was said and done, the dressmaker was able to fix it; the veil, however, had to go. I am sure all parents go through enormous stress when their daughters are about to be married. However, compared to Laura's other adventures, this was nothing.

Was She Always Tall?

In spite of clothing malfunctions, Laura's wedding was wonderful. Laura and Ray have a lovely home and two beautiful children, Mary Grace and Hampton, who were often curious about their parents. As teenagers, they are both beyond beautiful and both tall, taking after their equally beautiful six-foot one-inch mother.

• • •

"Tell us a little about Mom," they would ask. "Was she always tall?" I smiled when I replied, "Yes, your mother was born tall." They looked at me with puzzled faces. "What do you mean, born tall?"

• • •

Susan was well over nine months along, and it was time. We had sat through Lamaze training, but it turns out the real performance was nothing like the class. Yet there I was in the delivery room, having been invited to watch my wife give birth to our child. If I expected a Norman

5

Rockwell event, with the husband and wife holding hands, doctor and nurses gently smiling, and the process resulting in a beautiful baby babbling on Susan's stomach, I was to be quickly cured. I had no idea there would be so much groaning, grunting, pushing, and panting. Perhaps I wasn't ready for the decidedly unladylike positions Susan was forced to endure, or the difficulty of a breech birth, but I was prepared to use my Lamaze training and be of great assistance during the delivery. As if!

As we were puffing and pushing together, although to this day I don't know why I was doing that, it seemed

the birth was progressing well. After all, I heard the doctor calmly say, "That's good, keep pushing, the baby is coming." But then, his words came a little more quickly, "Yes, she's coming, almost there, oh my, she's still coming . . . my God, STOP PUSHING!" When Laura Elizabeth Armitage finally tumbled into the world, she clocked in at 24 inches long.

I do believe she was the longest, skinniest kid that doctor and nurse had ever delivered. My daughter, my firstborn, was two feet tall! If a child is two feet tall at birth, how high would she be when she stopped growing? When she was gingerly laid on Susan's stomach, she didn't fit. When I picked her up, she folded into an upside-down V. It's tough to cuddle a kid who is almost as tall as you are.

• • •

As I was telling the tale, Mary Grace and Hampton, who were already both tall, looked at each other with raised eyebrows. However, as they envisioned their Mom lurching in a stroller or falling out of their grandfather's arms, they grinned like Cheshire cats. "Really? I bet people stared at her for being so tall," they said. "Oh, that was nothing compared to her birthmark." They sat back and listened for a while longer.

• • •

The Birthmark

Although Laura was beautiful, she just kept getting longer. She was looking a little like a squeezed toothpaste container. I must admit to being just slightly frustrated pushing a tot in a stroller whose feet kept dragging on the ground. Her first pair of baby shoes had holes from their constant dangling on the sidewalk. The last thing she needed was something else to draw attention to her.

Yet, there it was, a dark red birthmark, looking like a bullet hole right between her eyes. We understood that the mark was only superficial, because the doctor told us so, and what new parents didn't believe their doctor? He also said it would likely disappear by the time she was three, but neither of us believed that for a second. Complete strangers would stare at her, then at us, trying to determine which parent was responsible. After the hundredth nosy questioner inquired as to this unfortunate mark, I became somewhat exasperated. The next inquisitor was greeted by a whispered tale of adventure and intrigue. "Laura had been shot between the eyes and had made a spectacular recovery; the only lingering reminder was the small bullet lodged just beneath her skin," I murmured dramatically. She looked at Laura, then at me, and back at Laura again, turned heel and muttered something about crime and punishment. Slowly, the

gunshot wound started to fade and sure enough, it totally disappeared when she was a little over three years old. My stories became far less exciting and a good deal less crime-ridden.

• • •

At this point Mary Grace and Hampton were wondering just what kind of father would say that about his daughter. They were also wondering about their mother. "Did she do anything else we should know?" That's when I told them about The Bottle.

• • •

The Bottle

What would parents do without pacifiers? To Susan and me, the pacifier was the most magical piece of rubber ever invented. It seemed it was the only device in the entire world that could quell Laura's crying, particularly when she awoke at night. As much as we worshiped that sucker, I cussed and cursed it almost equally. Every night the sobs would come, every night I would slowly trudge across the hall, half-asleep, then crawl under her crib and try to find the darn thing in the dark. With a sigh of relief, I would then plant it back into her bawling mouth. With the pacifier, we were able to get a little sleep while Laura had a "friend" to soothe her at night. However, perhaps we didn't realize how much she loved her friend.

As she became older, Laura replaced the pacifier with a plastic baby bottle, perhaps with some water, but very often quite empty. For me, this was a good thing because it tended to remain in the confines of her bed and I wasn't groping under the crib quite as often. We knew full well

that she would soon give it up after a reasonable amount of time, but it turns out we were a little optimistic.

Not only was the bottle her pacifier at night, she began to walk around with it during the day, even though most of the time the thing was empty. We had simply changed a small pacifier for a larger—and definitely uglier—one. Being made of plastic, it was scratched, discolored, and altogether quite disgusting—the kind of thing only a child could love. Weren't kids supposed to love beat-up old teddy bears or blankets?

At this point we decided to read Dr. Spock. After all, he was the expert on raising a child at the time, and like all parents of first children, we actually believed him. The good doctor warned of the great damage that bottles wrought on teeth and palate. We were young and clueless and had no doubt that our child would grow up with bad teeth, distorted lips, a lisp, and other Spockian damage, all because of a fifty-cent piece of plastic. It was time for tough love. We decided to take it away!

· · ·

Mary Grace and Hampton were staring at me like kids listening to a ghost story around a campfire. With large eyes, they asked, "What happened?"

· · ·

After three solid days and nights of crying and carrying on, Plan B seemed to be in order. Unfortunately, we didn't have a Plan B. However, given that parents were obviously smarter than children, we knew we could come up with something. I had an idea: Maybe we could cut the bottle in half! We suggested to Laura that if the bottle was cut, she could use the bottom part for a cup and together we would throw the top half away. She could even help me do the sawing.

As a three-year-old, Laura thought this a grand idea. We went down to the dingy basement, and equipped with an old hacksaw, we began the surgical procedure. Her eyes started to bulge a little as we cut through, but when the job was finished, she gingerly placed the top half in the garbage pail and took the "cup" upstairs for some juice. We even made it through the night without excessive pain. Mom and I patted ourselves on the back and decided that this child-raising stuff was not so tough after all. The next day, however, Laura emerged with one arm longer than the other.

She had trundled downstairs, fished through the garbage, retrieved the top, and jammed it over her right hand. She looked just like Captain Hook, except he didn't suck on his protruding finger. While she was proud as could be, we were hardly pleased. Watching a three-and-a-half-year-old, three-foot-tall child running around the house sucking on an artificial hand hardly built confidence in our parenting. To be fair, the extension was not an all-day thing; she put on her prosthesis only when she was tired or perhaps bored. However, it went everywhere she did, from trips in the car to trips to bed. It was near and very dear to her. That our friends looked at her a little strangely was not the problem.

• • •

"What was the problem?" they asked. "Did she lose it again?"
"No," I replied, "The problem was school!"

• • •

We were concerned that when Laura started kindergarten, she might be expelled for wearing a bottle to school (likely a breach of the dress code). We mentioned this possible dilemma a number of times, but Laura did not seem overly concerned. Then one day, out of the blue, just after we had celebrated her fourth birthday with her and The Bottle, she announced she would throw it away when she turned five.

This was a huge pronouncement. Although we felt we would have to saw the thing off her arm in order to get rid of it, we agreed to wait. Every other week we reminded her of her promise and she nodded solemnly, then went

about her business. On the morning of her fifth birthday, she quietly walked to the garbage pail and gently placed The Bottle into the bin and out of her life. Watching her at that moment, Susan and I realized that everything has its time, and no amount of "parenting" is going to change it. We were so proud of her, our eyes welled up like someone watching a sappy Hallmark movie. From then on, we knew Laura had vast inner strength which would serve her well later in her life.

• • •

"Did she really leave it in the garbage, really?" "Yes, she did—once your mother made up her mind, she followed through." Hamp and Mary Grace smiled at each other, affirming that based on their experiences, that was definitely so. We took a break, but a few weeks later, they cornered me again. They were still thinking of the discarded bottle, and they could not *help themselves. That's when they asked, "What else did Mom do—did she do any other crazy things?" I poured myself a cup of coffee, smiled, and said, "Well, she was quite the camper," then paused before adding, "And quite the meteorologist." With that, story time began again.*

• • •

Camping Out

Laura did not like loud noises. When she was about three years old, she was awakened by a tremendous clap of thunder. From that night on, she would wake up if it was too light, too dark, too quiet, too noisy, or if too many stuffed animals were in her bed. Thus began a new ritual. Every night, she would wander across the hall with her favorite blanket and climb into bed between Susan and me. This was cute for about three nights.

We quickly found that love of child did not include freezing little feet or a long, lanky body stretched diagonally across us, forcing me to the edge of the bed with one hand pressed against the floor for balance. Laura bounced out of bed at six in the morning, before Susan and I had wearily realigned ourselves like old car axles, only to be brutally reawakened by this bright-eyed, well-rested child. As thoughts of bad parenting knocked about my sleep-deprived mind, it was obvious this had to stop. We needed yet another plan.

We told her that if she really wanted to stay with us, she had to sleep on the floor. We had left Dr. Spock on the bookshelf, knowing he would not agree with our method. We stashed a beat-up old sleeping bag and pillow in our closet, and let her know that was to be her bed away from bed. Amazingly, that did the trick.

In the middle of the night, the little footsteps could be heard, then out of the closet would come The Bed. She rearranged things to her satisfaction, and remarkably, we all would have a fine sleep. Undoubtedly, there is something magical in old sleeping bags—they have that unique smell of campfire, rotting leaves, and mildew that kids seem to love. To this day, I remember the sound of a favorite blanket being dragged across the hall, the shadowy figure of a long child with a half-bottle screwed over her hand, and the smelly sleeping bag being pulled from its dark storage place to the floor beside the bed.

Comforting children is much easier when you are asleep beside them than when you are awake among them.

• • •

The kids just laughed at that; it turned out that when they were young, both of them often "camped" with their parents at night. "So that's where we got the dislike of loud noises."

"But weren't you still in Canada then—how did you get to Georgia?" I had to stop then as I remembered how we thought we had scarred our eldest daughter for life.

• • •

Life Changes in a Heartbeat

In today's academic climate, it takes months—if not years—of preparation to be accepted to graduate school. When I finished my master's work at the University of Guelph, I had no intention of continuing my education. However, in August, the adage about "The best-laid plans . . ." reared its head, and those well-laid plans became no plan at all. After a series of anxious phone calls, I received an interview at Michigan State University and days later was accepted for a doctoral program in its horticulture program. Such happenings could never occur today, but a new path for the family had appeared. However, I had to report to the University that week, and I left Susan and the kids behind.

Soon after, I frantically called Susan to tell her that she had to come to East Lansing to sign papers for housing, and that I had found an opening for Laura at the public school. She needed to bring her right way. Laura was five, already enrolled in her new school in Guelph and making a few friends, slowly. The very next day Susan went to her school, disenrolled her, packed her and her sister in the car, and left that life behind. Laura could not even bid her friends farewell; to them it was as if she vanished. To say that we felt extraordinarily guilty was to put it mildly.

Much later, when Laura was a young woman and this conversation would arise, she did not recall the drive from Canada at all. At the time, however, we believed she would definitely exhibit some form of trauma. Perhaps that was why she became a five-year-old meteorologist.

The Weather Girl

Moving is always a tough time for everyone, and it certainly was particularly difficult for a shy, tall girl who found herself at a new school in a new country. She just wanted to stay home. If she had to go out, she wished to be invisible. Staying at home was not possible as she was about to start kindergarten in a new school. Staying invisible was going to be difficult.

As concerned as we were with moving Laura, she was doing remarkably well in her new school. She had given up her bottle, and although she was the tallest in her class by far, she appeared to be coping with life's little crises just fine. Her sister Heather had arrived in the world just before we left Canada, and although she howled and talked constantly, she provided wonderful companionship. Everything was going far too well—we knew something was going to happen. Sure enough, The Drill occurred.

It never dawned on us that we were moving from a fairly calm area of Ontario to Michigan, which is occasionally visited by tornadoes. Nor did it occur to us to explain to Laura the facts of Midwestern weather. Laura was sitting at her desk when she experienced her first tornado drill at school. Without doubt, a tornado drill is simply another word for a subtle form of child abuse. Being told to dive under a desk while holding her hands over her head can scare any child half to death, and Laura was essentially traumatized. She had never heard of tornadoes in her old home and quickly decided she wanted nothing to do with them. The weather girl was born!

• • •

Mary Grace stopped me right there. She said that she too had always been frightened of the weather, then looked at me and said, "Maybe that's why when I was hugging Mom, she was hugging me just as hard." I replied, "Think of a timid five-year-old girl huddling under a desk, and you will understand."

• • •

When her teacher asked the children to learn their home phone numbers, she was most upset when she realized the first telephone number Laura memorized was the weather number, our home number being a distant second. She was terrified of dark clouds, and when the sky was even a little overcast, off she went to phone the weather. If she couldn't get through, she refused to go to school. If the day dawned overcast and gray, she developed a sore throat. And, oh my, if there was rain in the forecast, she contracted the bubonic plague. To this day, Laura has always been an early riser, more than likely because she always scrambled out of bed to watch the 6:00 a.m. weather on television. During our time in Michigan, if we wanted a long-range forecast, all we had to do was ask Laura. Thank goodness we never did have a tornado, but if one had been forecast, we would have been the first to know.

What Happened to the Time?

It was just yesterday that I was thinking how fast we were all growing up—Laura discarding her sawed-off bottle, me progressing in my job. The little girl who hated even answering the phone has become a speech pathologist, helping people every day.

Then one day she is getting married. What happened to the time? As we watched Laura continue her life's journey, we too approached our next phase, and not without a little trepidation.

We could look back and realize even though we had no idea what we were doing, we must have done something right. She became the girl every family would covet, the woman every man would like to marry, the caregiver every patient would wish for. We were so proud it hurt. I was also a little sad knowing that I had been relegated to second place as the most important man in her life.

But not without a little help here and there.

The genes of her grandparents she never met, those of her uncles and aunts, and the DNA of her mother and father linked up just right in our daughter. Her future will be one of family and career, and ours will hopefully include rocking grandchildren and watching them grow to young adults. They will be off to a good start; they will have chosen their mother well.

• • •

After reading this passage, her sister, who also has a family of her own, just smiled and said, "Dad, you make her out to be such a Girl Scout. If you knew of some of the adventures she got into in high school, you and Mom would have gone crazy!" I locked eyes with Heather and replied calmly that any stories that she did not share were likely not shared for a reason.

• • •

• • •

As soon as Heather left, I picked up the phone. "Laura, your sister tells me you may have had a few escapades in high school you didn't share." Silence.

"And for that, your mother and I thank you."

• • •

HEATHER

Laura would not be the person she is without the interactions of her sister and brother. That's just the way families evolve. And oh my, how they evolved. Today, Laura's younger sister Heather and her husband David are raising a rather large family. In fact, they have four highly spirited children. Drew, Ben, Will, and Kate are now teenagers and like their mother are handsome, creative and curious, and like their mother, a wee bit crazy. If one word could describe their lifestyle, it would be Chaos with a capital C. At times when we were zigging and zagging to get out of the way, I thought I could hear David mumbling in the background, "I didn't sign up for this."

On one visit prior to the teenage years, Susan and I pulled into the driveway, already girded for the pandemonium that was sure to lie ahead. Even before we got out of the car, the front door of the house opened and the dog shot out, Heather yelling at it to return. Then Ben flew out of the house and gave chase down the street shouting at the dog. While the road was not a major thoroughfare, nor was it a quiet cul-de-sac. Susan already had her head in her hands.

Seeing that her family was rapidly disappearing, Heather cussed and started her car down the drive, only to see Will running alongside, trying to open the door beside her. As she accelerated further, Kate, not to be left behind, raced after the car as it motored down the street. By this time, Susan was in heart attack mode. I had to exit

our car, if only to watch the train wreck unfold. There in the front yard, nonchalantly tossing a ball up and down was Drew, the eldest. "Don't worry, they'll be back soon, this happens all the time. Want to toss a football?" Sure enough, Heather soon returned, dog and kids in tow. After muttering something unprintable, Heather joined me in extricating her mother from the car.

Such is my daughter's life, but as often as we cringe at the bedlam, we also look at each other in amazement—she is Supermom. She seems able to take every calamity in stride, and still appear composed. She has surely mellowed with age, because things were not always quite so calm.

In the Beginning

Heather, David, and their family live about two hours east of us, so we are able to visit often. As the grandkids grew up, the bedlam was quieter and we were able to sit together—at least for a few minutes—before the fighting started. During one of our visits, Heather had enough and shouted, "Will you kids be quiet? You are always telling each other what to do!"

I didn't mean to laugh during this stern confrontation, but couldn't help myself. I had to explain that they came by their talking honestly. "Your mother was put on this earth to keep everyone straight. If we wanted to know anything about anything or anybody, we simply asked your mom." They stopped their squabbling and looked up. "She spoke more words by the time she was five than the rest of the family combined. As the middle child, she constantly reminded us that 'the filling is the best part of the sandwich.'"

• • •

Her children nodded in agreement. "That's Mom all right." Then I added, "We realized she would not be ignored when she was sent to the children's hospital immediately after she was born." Like a popped cork, there was no going back, and later Kate asked, "What did you mean about Mom when you said she gave you a scare at the hospital?" We got ourselves comfortable and I replied, "Well, I was probably more frightened than anyone, however, it was there her reputation began."

• • •

A Gentle Reminder

Heather was born active. She entered the world with lungs full of air, which she emptied in deafening fashion at every possible opportunity. When she was delivered, I counted ten fingers and ten toes, and given her leather lungs, I knew that we were blessed to have a healthy child. However, she developed a rather high fever, and while I was a little worried, Susan was beside herself.

This was not difficult to understand. Our first child, Shannon, was born on June 18, 1971 and died 24 hours later. No one can prepare you for a loss of a child; no one can understand what a mother goes through when such a tragedy occurs. Friends and family were supportive but Susan experienced major depression. It is not so much the initial tragedy that consumes you—everyone was stunned and arrangements kept us busy. It was the weeks and months after her death that were the hardest. Life seems to stop; there is no understanding of the whys and wherefores, and although people around us did their best, we were alone within a black cloud of despair. I remember Susan remarking that some of her hardest times were not reliving it with friends who came to comfort her, but times when friends were so afraid of upsetting her that they never mentioned the baby. She remarked that if ever she met a mother under similar circumstances, she would go out of her way to talk to her. Pretending it did not occur or speaking about everything but her loss was far worse than talking about what happened. Unfortunately, friends and colleagues have experienced similar loss, and Susan has been there to comfort them. A number of years later, when Susan went to nursing school, she became a labor and delivery nurse.

Needless to say, any issue with a newborn child was cause for great concern, and frightened the heck out of us. The nurses and doctors were not concerned, but due to Susan's anxiety, our newborn was immediately transferred to the Sick Children's Hospital in Montreal.

Watching your two-day-old baby taken to a strange hospital where only the sickest of children were treated has to be one of the most traumatic experiences for any parent; we were no exceptions.

Susan could not visit so I went to the intensive care ward alone. There I experienced firsthand the sights and sounds of very sick children. Incubators and tiny cribs contained miniature people, most of whom were wired to monitors and instruments larger than them. With beeps and bells, electrodes and diodes, monitors and buttons, sturdy technology and fragile babies existed side by side. To me, young and naïve as I was, it was a Dantesque environment. As I walked through the area, I couldn't help but notice that many of the babies were lying slightly elevated, their mattresses held up by a short wooden support. As I passed one of these tiny people, a buzzer

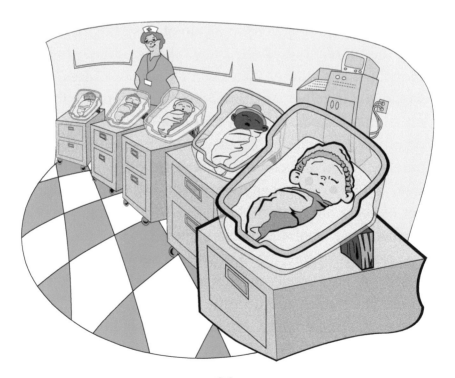

over her head suddenly shrilled. I jumped in shock and realized something must be terribly wrong. Staring at the screaming monitor, I found myself frozen in place for what seemed an eternity but probably lasted less than 5 seconds. When I think about what happened next those many years ago, I am still a little incredulous.

Ignoring my presence, the duty nurse calmly walked over and delivered a quick but efficient blow to the support block, causing the little person to come crashing down. The jolt caused a tiny wail from the child and the buzzing stopped. The nurse realigned the support block and with a little smile at me, went on about her other business. Snapping out of my paralysis, I asked her what had happened. "Many of these children are so premature, some of their vital responses aren't well developed. They need a little reminder every now and then to do some of the more important things, like breathe."

To me, this was a miracle. The baby's breathing had stopped and the jolt of falling was sufficient to get the lungs expanding again! It was a fascinating mix of crude technology (a wooden block?) combined with state-of-the-art monitors and alarms, merged with good old-fashioned nursing. Every now and then, when I see my children running around, I wonder if another active child somewhere knows how a small block of wood and a calm karate chop reminded him to live. I also wondered at the time what the heck Heather was doing there.

• • •

The kids stared at me and said, "Really, a wooden block? Did mom have one of those too, was she that sick?" I smiled in

27

remembrance, and said, "It turned out she was as healthy as could be, and she was always hungry."

• • •

Yelling for the Milkman

One of the things that struck me as strange in the hospital was the lack of childlike noises. Machines were humming and an occasional monitor was buzzing, but few children were crying. Perhaps many were fighting so hard for their lives that crying simply was not important enough to waste time or energy on. There was, however, a notable exception. Over in the corner of the ward, off the beaten path, was Heather, telling all who would listen that she did not belong there. And oh, how the nurses enjoyed listening. Her obvious tenacious hold on life was a thrill to all. They were used to children barely clinging to it.

Of course, she was hungry! One of the reasons I went to the hospital was to deliver her food. Susan had started to nurse Heather immediately after birth. Since mother and daughter could not be united, it was up to Dad to play milkman and deliver the breast milk. I had delivered many things in my day, from newspapers to chocolate bars, but I never had any inclination to deliver breast milk. Ah, the immaturity of youth.

The first time I was so embarrassed, driving bottles of newly-gathered breast milk in a Styrofoam container through the streets of Montreal. I was sure I was the only father who had ever done this and equally sure everyone knew the exact contents of the "picnic basket." I delivered the white gold to one of the nurses who simply said

"thank you," took the container, and left me standing there feeling very embarrassed about my embarrassment. My career as a milkman continued for only a few more days, as it was obvious Heather belonged with her mother. Ironically, not only was she the healthiest of all the newborns, she also steadfastly refused to nurse anyway.

• • •

The kids were a little embarrassed thinking about their mother breastfeeding, so the grandkids and I decided to take a walk. It was a cold winter's day in Augusta and everyone bundled up. After hearing the kids complain about being cold, I could not help myself. "When your mother was a kid in Canada, this was a cool summer's day!" They snickered, as all kids do, when they hear about the old days, but a few minutes later, Drew asked, "Why did you leave Canada—why are we all in Georgia?"

• • •

On a Park Bench in Ottawa

Our time in Guelph was coming to an end. I had somehow managed decent grades and after two eventful years was about to graduate. The Question then raised its head: "What now?" During my time there, I had completed a small project with the Canadian government, and upon graduating I was asked to fill a horticulturist position in Ottawa.

It was a fine offer, involving managing some of the greenhouses that supplied plants for the grounds as well as cut flowers for formal dinners with heads of state hosted by Prime Minister Pierre Trudeau and his wife, Maggie. My main responsibility, however, was the "greening of government buildings." The mid 1970s ushered in the realization that large buildings need not be barren and bereft of nature. Essentially, I was to coordinate efforts with the foliage industry, interior designers, and architects to make these buildings greener. And they were even going to pay me!

I visited Ottawa and was shown through the building that would be my office, and walked around building after building and through the many greenhouses realizing that this was a huge job. I was excited!

• • •

"Wow," said Drew. "The Prime Minister of Canada! Mom has never mentioned anything about Ottawa. What happened—did you take it?"

• • •

I was excited but Susan seemed to have some reservations. She said there was something that did not feel right, and she asked me to put off signing a contract until we could visit the capitol together. Ottawa is a beautiful city: clean, efficient, and a wonderful place to raise children. It was only two hours from Montreal and family, and it seemed to me an excellent opportunity.

Susan and I made the trip to Ottawa and after some time, we found ourselves sitting on a bench, looking downtown. She had been rather pensive, then she asked, "Where is your office?" I pointed to a tall building just down the road. "What floor will you work on?" "The 19th," I replied. "Will you have to wear a tie?" "Yes," I said.

She looked at me and said, "Don't take the job."

She tried to tell me that my strengths were with people, with teaching, and getting my hands dirty. All this time we were sitting on a bench, she was explaining to me who I was. It was rather embarrassing. But she was right. "Something else will come our way, but this is not the right choice—you will be miserable." And just like that, I turned down the job, the money, and our future as I had seen it.

Earning a master's degree was an accomplishment to be sure, but I was effectively now an overeducated, unemployed young man, and not so young at that, and with few expectations. I scrambled, calling every university I knew, in Canada and the States, and miracle of miracles, I was invited to work on my doctorate at Michigan State University.

For a while there, we actually believed we knew what we were doing, but life seems to find a way of writing its own script. There we were, packing boxes and crates and wondering what to do with items that suddenly became an expense rather than a keepsake.

Many years later, Heather and David decided to move across town in Augusta, and I mentioned the idea of a garage sale. Heather looked up and cried out, "I will never have a garage sale—I still remember my pink elephant!" and immediately left the room.

• • •

Her kids stopped everything and asked, "What does Mom mean, her pink elephant?" "Well," I replied, "It started out as a pretty routine garage sale, and then it wasn't."

• • •

The Garage Sale

Who invented the garage sale? Why would anyone spend hours readying leftovers at fire sale prices only to have complete strangers demand them for even less? However, more than one friend told us that a garage sale can be a wonderful family adventure, while teaching kids a little about economics and finance. I didn't believe them for a second, but we decided to give it a go.

What better way to get rid of those accumulated useless possessions that none of us were using any longer? It is said that "One man's ceiling is another man's floor." Our ceiling had its fair share of junk, and hopefully we could find someone's floor to dump it on. We were flying around every which way putting ridiculously low prices on items which were once important enough to buy for ridiculously high prices. Laura and Heather got into the spirit. They decided to part with a few things they were no longer using, and the idea of making a dime or quarter was incentive enough to go through their toy box. We rounded up old furniture, games with pieces missing, wrinkled paperbacks, dusty lamps, dented bicycles, and every description of used clothing. Laura spent a great deal of time thinking just what she would keep or part with, and added a few things to the table. Heather, on the other hand, who was almost four years old, had thoughts of big money rolling in. We questioned her as she brought down half a dozen stuffed animals and assorted other playthings. For Heather to bring out her animals was surprising. Her bed was a naturalistic landscape of animals of all descriptions, sizes, and colors, each with a special name. "Yes, I'm sure, I don't play with these anymore," she announced as she cast them on the pile. We should have known.

Those innocents who naively advertise garage sales in the local paper don't know about the professional garage sale hunters lurking out there. These folks do nothing on weekends but cruise neighborhoods looking for bargains, arriving at least one hour before you are ready and demanding to know prices of things that aren't even for sale. I could have sold my house and children to these people as long as I sold them for a penny on the dollar. In truth, our once-precious possessions were not sufficiently interesting, and they soon departed. Then we waited for the onrush.

It turns out that garage sales should actually be called fire sales, and after a few hours, it was pretty obvious the sale was not going well, and we were all a little tired and frustrated. Except Heather. She looked at the event as a challenge, and decided to add a few more things, figuring that if the volume increased, so would the cash. She carried some badly torn comic books, a few old pieces of clothing, and four more stuffed animals to the table. Her latest consisted of a blue and green turtle, a white and red rabbit, a small brown bear, and her cute pink elephant. When I asked again if she wouldn't miss them, she was her usual decisive self and had no second thoughts at all. By 11:00 that morning, more people were wandering around and, unbelievably, our junk was starting to sell.

As the day wore on, we noticed Heather becoming more and more agitated as other children and assorted parents considered her potpourri of items. Whenever anyone approached her table, her eyes narrowed and she began to fidget, particularly when her animals were

34

examined. However, she soon tired of manning her station and wandered away. She returned just in time to see a little girl and her mother leaving the house with Heather's pink elephant lovingly tucked under the girl's arm. When she saw her "friend" leaving, her face utterly crumbled and it was obvious that her worse fears had been realized. She gritted her teeth, tried to be stoic, and looked like she might be all right.

However, as the situation became more obvious, grief stricken, she raced down the driveway crying, "No, no, that's MY elephant!" Her eyes were red, her tears were flowing, and she was running with determined desperation. The elephant's new owner glanced out the rear window of the departing car and wondered why some child was chasing their car down the road. Our youngest daughter could do nothing but watch a part of her life disappear in a red station wagon. She was crushed, as were we! With rivulets of tears rolling down her cheeks, she silently gathered the rest of her animals together and went inside. We tried to console her but were ineffective. We reasoned that she would soon forget about

35

the elephant and that day. It turns out that she never forgot the feeling of knowing that something was gone forever, never to return. In fact, she reminded us of her loss when she was a teenager, and if the subject of garage sales comes up, we hear about it yet again. We have had a number of garage sales since then. However, if you are looking for stuffed animals at ridiculously low prices, you won't find any at our house.

• • •

The kids ran into the kitchen and asked Heather, "Is that true, Mom? Do you really remember your pink elephant?" She looked up at her children, thought for a few seconds, and replied, "Yes, I really do."

• • •

The health of our kids is always in the back of every parent's mind, but knock on wood, Laura had never suffered more than normal childhood ailments. When Susan was applying a salve or bandage to her finger or leg after a fall or minor mishap, we seldom thought twice about it.

However, our second child seemed to be the most accident-prone kid I have ever known. I suppose a few misfortunes are to be expected—no one is accident free. Perhaps it was because she was always on the move, but with Heather, we were in emergency rooms far too often.

If There Was a Pin to Step On

I am embarrassed that we called Heather the "Drama Queen." As we laughed with friends about kids and grandkids many years later, it turns out that every family has at least one drama queen. But back then, we were still learning. The term seemed to fit; every time something occurred, especially when she was very young, she made sure we all knew. When the shrieking started this time, even though it sounded apocalyptic, we trotted, rather than raced to the latest calamity.

This time, the screams came from the stairs where Heather had been bounding up and down with exhausting energy. Our baby girl was crumpled in a heap, sobbing and pointing to her foot. The good news: Heather had finally found Susan's missing sewing needle—we had been looking for it for days. The bad news: it was protruding from her foot. I suppose it did look rather gruesome, but it was only a sewing needle. However, the closer we looked, the more we understood the sobbing and the cries. It had gone right through the bottom of her foot to the top and was visible on both sides. Even though it appeared to have entered cleanly and didn't bury itself in bone, we thought someone with a bit more training should take a look. So off we went, carrying a sobbing child, to one of our many visits to emergency rooms, this time to have a needle excised and a wound caressed. A few hours later, she was home with crutches and a bandaged foot, both of which persisted for about a day. After that, we just hoped life would be a little less dramatic for a while. We were living in Michigan at the time, and things seemed to be progressing well. What harm could come from grabbing a treat at the local Burger Doodle?

• • •

I didn't tell tales every time we would see the grandkids, but stories simply presented themselves when we went to cer-

tain places. With Heather's great brood, a fast food visit every now and then was essential. This time, however, I stopped dead in my tracks when I spied those awful round stools, attached to equally gruesome plastic tables. Something must have come over my face, because Drew looked at me and asked, "Is something wrong?" As we sat I replied to my now rapt audience, "It was a place just like this that your mother lost her teeth . . ."

• • •

Disaster at the Burger Doodle

Who would put rotating chairs in a restaurant visited by children? What child would simply sit in one and spin peacefully? They basically call out to children to stand up and twirl on them, at least they did to daughter number two. When I saw those chairs, something in the back of my mind shouted a warning, soon ignored by the mind-numbing line-standing prospect of ordering a meal that I knew my stomach would soon regret. While jostling for position to order indigestion, I neglected to see where my daughter had wandered.

Slow motion! That's how people see events when something really bad is unfolding. Even from the jostling line, I saw her across the room—dancing, singing, and twirling atop one of those gruesome green stools. Catastrophe was imminent!

Most kids fall on their hands or elbows, perhaps their heads, but not Heather. She hit the enameled table squarely with her front teeth. As I watched and heard her land on her mouth, and as she screamed while the entire restaurant went quiet, once again, I realized how awful a parent I was. This time there was no trotting. I raced to the

hospital with my bloody child sobbing in my arms, hoping for no major damage to Heather and for forgiveness for me. The emergency room doctor solemnly informed us that she had not lost her teeth, but there was significant damage. So, with her teeth secured in her bandaged mouth, Heather left the emergency room once again.

• • •

As I was relating the story, I could see the kids feeling their mother's pain. But all they could say, almost in unison was, "What happened next?" "The worst part," I replied. "The absolute worst."

• • •

Perhaps we had dodged a bullet, and I prayed with all my might that the necessary visit to the specialist would be somewhat routine. After all, they were baby teeth. We were not referred to our kind family dentist, but faced someone whose title was enough to scare us, The Pediatric Orthodontist. After a lengthy examination, he took us aside and asked how something like this could happen. If words were ice, I would have been frozen on the spot as Susan related my parental incompetence. Even in this barrage of indictments, I was hoping I had not disfigured my daughter for life. I knew my optimism was misguided when The Pediatric Orthodontist stared at me and said that Heather would need two root canals.

Root canals are bad enough for anyone, but for a young child, they are particularly traumatic. Believing that these were baby teeth that would fall out anyway, and thinking of the pain our daughter would have to endure, we went back and forth with the dentist. Sheer folly! However, we could not ignore his reasoning that the damage, if not repaired, would likely result in a bad outcome later. First Laura's mouth was in danger of permanent damage with the pacifier, and now her sister's jaw, teeth, and smile were also about to be marred. That we could not even come close to affording it never entered the conversation—we said yes.

The root canals turned out to be a wise decision. The procedures were awful, for everyone, but the resiliency of youth played a huge factor in Heather's quick recovery. As to her front teeth, one turned yellow and discolored but the other was saved. They remained in place to provide a template for her permanent front teeth, both of which emerged in fine fashion on her sixth birthday. The only reminder of her fall was a temporary gap in her new teeth. We still frequent Burger Doodle joints here and there, and I cannot do so without remembering that hideous plastic furniture. However, one glimpse of Heather's pretty smile quickly dispels any additional thoughts of spinning stools.

Gathering Shells

While Heather was collecting scars like trophies on a shelf and Laura was cowering under chairs in her Michigan school, I was in school as well. Unfortunately, my studies at the university were not going particularly well. I was in over my head early in my studies, and to add insult to injury, I was one of the oldest students in the graduate class. I had a good deal of catching up to do to stay with the youngsters. It was obvious I was getting a little anxious when I suggested that Susan stop hanging curtains at our new house, since I was about to flunk out.

Somehow, I managed to scrape through the first couple years, with a large helping of support from my wife and some good luck to boot. School was a real business to me, with expectations in the classroom, the lab, and my job in the research greenhouse. When the children were asked what their daddy's job was, they replied, "He goes to school." That was the only job they had known their father to have. Coming home from work every day to a family was the real reason I succeeded. Flunking out was not an option! And as the kids became a little older, I started to believe that their misadventures may have been behind them.

. . .

Many years later, when we sat around with friends recounting family stories, such a statement was greeted with laughter. "So, what really happened next?" they asked. After a brief pause, I conceded, "Well, Heather was not content with misadventures at home—she even found a way to meet emergency room doctors at the lake.

. . .

Susan was meeting new friends and getting involved in the public schools, and Laura and Heather were turning out pretty normal even though we had yanked them away from family and their homeland. Everything seemed to be going well in their father's education, however, soon enough, it was time to sit for the oral examinations for my doctorate in horticulture. There is little debate that this is one of the worst experiences in a graduate student's life. It all seems a little medieval. One student sits in a room facing half a dozen accomplished professors, each one assessing the student's ability to continue with the program. If you fail, you are gone! If one truly wants to experience pain and agony, one only has to subject oneself to a four-hour pasting from a bushwhacking gang of tenured professors. In every such gang, there is a member whose sole reason for attending is to shoot off his guns of useless knowledge for everyone in the room to hear. Each takes a turn trying to impress the others while at the same time seeing how much the student can squirm. The squirm factor is very important in an oral examination. The student needs to show a respectable amount of squirming in front of his elders, but not too much squirm or the hounds will start baying. Somehow, I survived!

Having endured this particularly macabre form of higher education, I was delighted when a friend offered us his lakefront cottage for a few days. It was off in the middle of nowhere, which seemed all the better. It was too good to be true. A sunny day in northern Michigan, a lovely cool lake, shoulders free of stress, Susan and I relaxing, watching the kids running in and out of the placid waves. Our minds were on sun and surf, not on our accident-waiting-to-happen daughter. Big mistake.

When Heather started screaming, our first thought was that she had probably jammed her toe on a rock or fallen in the water. Actually, my first thought was, "Oh, now what?" But on lifting her out of the water and seeing the blood flowing from her foot, we realized this was more than a stubbed pinkie. It was really bleeding! With her foot wrapped in bloody towels, we raced off to the county hospital, more than an hour away over hilly, twisting country roads. The drive was an absolute hell as night settled around us. We didn't know where we were, where we were going, or how to get there. No GPS, no 911, just an old map, an old car, and old roads. The towels were red and Heather was moaning the whole way. Laura and her mother were doing their best to soothe her, while I was praying the map was accurate. Finally arriving at the small, but obviously well-run hospital, Heather was whisked to the emergency room with Susan at her side. It turned out she had stepped on a broken clam shell and suffered a particularly deep and ragged cut. Laura and I sat outside the room. Neither of us will forget Heather's pain that night. The foot is a particularly tender part of the anatomy and when the doctor probed and cleaned it,

she was beside herself. Gut-wrenching cries (mine and Laura's) accompanied each injection of painkiller around the cut.

Laura and I were convinced that Heather's foot was being amputated or something equally gruesome. It was all I could do not to race into the treatment room and rescue my daughter from the obvious pain. The yells and screams soon subsided to a background of sobbing, but the sobbing was even harder to listen as it continued for what seemed an eternity. Heather finally hobbled out on one crutch, subdued but not defeated. The appearance of a tiny smile lit up the hospital corridor like quiet fireworks on a still night. The next morning, we headed back from the shortened holiday, our time shattered but our daughter intact. We never had the opportunity to visit that cottage again, but the scar on Heather's foot provides a constant reminder of its role in the life of a tough kid.

While enduring the normal scrapes and cuts of all active kids, she was bitten at least three times by dogs of poor dispositions. The fact that Heather loves dogs, and has two at home still remains a mystery to me.

As we got older, these seeming calamities receded in our memories. Heather bears no emotional scars and has no fear of lakes, shells, or rotating chairs. In fact, perhaps these accidents acted as a catalyst of her lack of fear in new situations. She was like the Pied Piper to her little friends, and went where others feared to tread—well, at least her big sister. As I look back, it seemed we were actually getting settled in, and perhaps no great misadventures lay ahead, at least not for a while. I probably should not have believed that.

Guess What?

The life and times of our small family, like any family, had its ups and downs, but a bit of predictability was evolving. It seems that I had been a student forever, dragging Laura and Susan from the West Island of Montreal to Guelph, Ontario, then along with Heather to East Lansing, Michigan. However, time was progressing and as the year was waning, we were doing just fine. It was a new year and to our resolutions we added hopes. Hopes for continued health, hopes for soon finishing my education, and hopes for actually getting a real job. We had no money and no idea what the future would bring, but we had two healthy children. As uncertain as our futures were, there was a semblance of routine in our nuclear family. However, early in the New Year, I knew there was be a problem when Susan sat me down. To any husband, the words "We need to talk." brings chills to his entire soul. But then Susan smiled. "Guess what? I'm pregnant."

Who Knew?

In spite of Heather's calamities, and my examinations, lectures, and thesis nightmares, our time in East Lansing flew by. Laura had recovered from her tornado traumas and the rest of us got on with our daily activities. While my time there was rewarding, it was time to find a job. So, résumé in hand, I hit the job market, and, of course, we first looked back to Canada.

Who knew? When all was said and done, there were no opportunities in the homeland. Yet, there in front of us was an offer to work at what was a truly up and coming academic institution, the University of Georgia.

The Big Move

When we originally left Canada, we certainly had no intention of working in the United States; in fact, I had no intention of going to school there. However, Michigan had turned out to be a pleasant place to live, and we had little fear of staying in the States for a few years if things did not work out at home. But the South?

The South was the last place we ever thought we would find ourselves. We knew as much about Georgia as Georgians knew about Canada, that is to say, embarrassingly little. Laura was eight, Heather was five, and Jon was just a bulge in Susan's stomach. As discussions about moving became more serious, we debated pros and cons, the unknowns, and the children's futures. We thought about leaving our friends and families, and considered all that could go wrong in this totally unknown place. The job offer was reassuring but we certainly could have gone back to Montreal to wait for something that would eventually turn up in the homeland.

When all was said and done, we abandoned the trepidation and angst that was crowding in, and I said, "Let's treat this as a two-year foreign assignment; hopefully there will be more opportunities to return to Canada after that. And working in Georgia will allow me to establish my academic credentials while taking us on a family adventure." Two years seemed about right, and so came the most momentous decision in this family's short history: we were going to move to a place called Athens, Georgia.

What Have I Done?

With a good deal of trepidation, we were about to live our lives in a new country, a new state, and with a new job. We must have been quite a sight: five-year-old

Heather, eight-year-old Laura, and a very pregnant and uncomfortable wife squeezed into a non-air-conditioned Chevy Citation, rolling down I-75. We arrived in Athens in late August to temperatures of at least 100F and 100% humidity. Oh my, what had I done?

Like children snowbound in a storm, we spent the first two weeks peering out the windows, not daring to go out and not believing anything or anybody could live out there.

School Down in the Land of Cotton

As in most turns in a family's life, the children assimilated the changes much better than the adults. However, it certainly was not easy for them either. A move is upsetting for everyone, but probably more so for a shy child whose only goal was to remain invisible. Seeing our grown-up and confident daughters today makes us forget that perhaps we all need a little help in overcoming life's traumas. We well remember sending our daughters off to their first days of school. For Laura and Heather, the first weeks of school during our "foreign assignment" turned out to be a unique experience.

• • •

Many years later, we were visiting Heather's mob of four teenagers and two dogs. The weather was awful, they were stuck inside, and all around was an off-key symphony of bickering and squabbling. It was not at all pleasant. Their mother had had enough, and they knew it. Norman Rockwell had left the building.

I held out my hands out and said, "Do you know that your mother can be one of the kindest people in the world?" They looked at me in disbelief and muttered something about Granddad being delusional, but Ben said, "What do you mean?"

• • •

Heather was always adaptable to change. Whoever penned the saying "Go with the flow" had Heather in mind. On the other hand, change was traumatic to Laura. Still feeling out of place with the other children, she took many months to become comfortable in new situations. When we told them that we were moving from Michigan to Georgia, neither was particularly pleased, but Laura hated the idea. She was eight years old and the thought of attending a new school terrified her. We felt awful.

When we met the teachers and principal at the school, we felt a little less guilty. They went out of their way to make the kids feel comfortable, they greeted us with respect and were obviously proud of their school. We felt much better about the move and the children's futures. However, as Laura quickly reminded us, we were not going to school, she was, and she didn't feel any better at all.

Our first contact was with Mrs. Peterson, the office secretary. She smiled at our eldest daughter and proceeded to pronounce her name with a honeyed southern accent, slowly and with the two syllables stretched out like toffee. "Welcome Laar-raaaah." she seemed to say. When Laura tried to correct her, this lovely southern lady simply said, "Don't worry, honey, you will be pronouncing it just like us by the end of the year." She was correct!

A Helping Hand
When You Least Expect It

Another experience in the near future terrified Laura. She had never taken a school bus before and was dreading such an unknown experience. Heather, who was starting kindergarten, couldn't wait to get on board.

We drove the two kids the first day. Heather ran off with a quick kiss to find her class, but Laura squeezed

Dad's hand tightly and fought off tears with every step toward the classroom. Once she was seated at her desk, we parted with the kind of heavy hearts that only parents who have left their kids "for their own good" can feel. Heather was bubbling after her first day, telling us about her classmates, teachers, and their funny way of talking. Laura's silence, however, said far more than Heather's chatter. Guilt has a way of rearing its head when things go badly. I had felt terrible enough about moving the family further from their Canadian roots but especially for exposing Laura to such trauma. Because the few weeks prior to school had passed smoothly and friendships were starting in the new neighborhood, I had stored up a little optimism that school might not be so bad, after all. It didn't go well at the beginning.

Laura would not go to the bus by herself, hated the idea of going to school, and could make no new friends there. We were more than a little concerned. We knew we should have simply said, "Get on with it, girl!" but neither of us was good at that tough love stuff.

One day as we were fretting about how Laura was coping, her sister walked up to me and said, "Don't worry, Dad, I've been taking her." Sure enough, Heather, who would have loved to run off to the bus and skip merrily to her new classroom, walked with Laura to the bus stop, and escorted her to her class, and met her again after school to get home. This seems like a small thing, but it was a gesture of love on Heather's part. Every day, for about four weeks, a small five-year-old took care to be sure her older sister arrived at class. Laura never asked, but there seemed to be an unspoken agreement between

the two. From our point of view, this was beyond amazing. Such cooperation was not at all normal. They often
fought like cats and dogs, and the term "sibling rivalry"
was one they helped popularize.

Although she still disliked school, Laura started
to adapt. Shoulders back (no more slouching to look
shorter), lips slightly bitten, she took her place each
day without complaint. It was about six months before
she became comfortable. We have no doubt that one of
the reasons she persevered was because of the quiet,
unasked-for help of her little sister. In the next few years,

we had numerous opportunities to leave Athens, but Laura would no sooner leave her new home than would a tiger lose its stripes. Neither of the kids talks much about those days, but I was as proud of Heather as I have ever been. Maybe she would grow up as a lawyer or politician and then really drive everyone crazy.

• • •

"Really, Mom?" the kids laughingly responded. "You really did that for Aunt Laura?" Heather too was quiet, perhaps thinking about those times many years ago. "I had completely forgotten about that." She then looked up at her kids and growled, "Don't believe a word of it, I'm still going to get you," and to their delight, ran after them all.

• • •

It's a Boy?

"It's a boy?" Heather was most upset she was not going to have a little sister, but the rest of us were ecstatic. By the fall, we were starting to get the hang of the weather and the neighborhood, and the arrival of our son put any inconveniences behind us. However, while life was hectic enough with Laura and Heather, it turns out the meaning of the word *chaos* had yet to be defined.

JONATHAN AKA BIG JON

Jonathan was born to a perfectly sane woman two nights before Halloween. The delivery went well, and mother and son soon returned to our new home. Laura and Heather were in school and I actually had a job. Compared to his sisters, Jon was really an easy baby. However, it turned out the first few years of his life were just a period for marking time, a parking spot if you will, for the entertainment he would provide as he grew up. Within three years, his mother and father were questioning their sanity and the girls looked like angels.

Like his oldest sister, Jon was tall. He was never huge or fat, just big. He was the one the photographer placed in the back row, and every year his school photograph came back with a face only. As I look at these old photos today, I am really not sure if he ever changed clothes from one picture to the next. All that is visible is a dirty collar. Sometimes I envied the fathers of the short kids; at least they get to see their entire child. But then again, when I recall the juice and snack stains down the front of his shirt, perhaps I should have given silent thanks for his size.

• • •

Today Jon and Mandy live with their young daughter Avery in Indiana. Unfortunately, visits are not frequent enough, but when the kids and grandkids get together, what a time they have. On one such occasion, Jonathan did something that made the kids laugh, and I said, "Jon, do you remember The Big Pinch?" Immediately, Susan started to laugh, Jon scratched his head, and in unison, Kate and Avery asked, "What was The Big Pinch?" I looked at them and replied, "It may have been your grand-mother's most embarrassing moment . . ."

• • •

Jon was not a bad kid, he simply found himself in situations where trouble was his closest companion. The girls had taught us that certain circumstances should be carefully avoided whenever possible, but with Jon, they appeared as if by spontaneous generation. On this particular day, things were progressing smoothly, which is to say that Jon had not yet broken anything or gotten into any serious trouble.

A few miles from our house was an old textile mill. Such mills were common in the South and by 1900, ninety-eight mills were operating in Georgia alone. After the Second World War, many disappeared overseas, but a few were still operating. Thomas Textiles was located on the banks of the North Oconee River, and was originally powered by a water mill. Built in 1829, it was but a shadow of itself by the time we moved to the area, but children's clothing was still being produced there. Twice a year, seconds of fabric and apparel were offered at bargain prices through their outlet store, equally small and equally aged. For three hundred and sixty-three days of the year, Thomas Textiles was a quiet place, but on bargain days, every woman in the entire state knew of the sale. For every one of them, it was a point of honor to be there at the opening bell. And two people wading into the horde on that day were Susan and a two-year-old boy.

• • •

I could see that my history of Georgia cotton mills was making Avery and Kate antsy, but with the last statement, they sat up and as one they said, "Okay, okay, but why was our grandmother so embarrassed?"

• • •

Women were poring over the clothes in a search and destroy mission which would have made the Army Rangers proud. Susan knew this was no place for a toddler but the bargains were too good to pass up. For the first fifteen minutes, Jon was the golden boy. However, boredom soon set in, and he wanted to wander around, play with clothes, and see what all the excitement was about. Not a good idea. He was in fact, in danger of being trampled. When Susan said no for the fourth time, Jon did what all two-year-olds did—he threw a temper tantrum.

Imagine this large small boy on a scruffy wooden floor crying and yelling things incomprehensible while waves of women stepped over him, jostling for position at the clothes table. But Susan was not taken aback; after all, this was not the first time she had encountered such behavior. From experience, she knew that the best response was no response, and she simply decided to ignore him. It worked at home.

Since she was being of no help, Jonathan had a plan. He decided to use the ultimate attention grabber. He calmly reached up and pinched Susan on the bottom, hard. This tactic had been successful before and likely would have been again, except for one small problem. It wasn't Susan's backside.

Above the noise and the din, a piercing shriek was heard by one and all. Big Jon had applied one of his finest efforts to the ample bottom of a woman nearby. She rose to heights never again attainable in her lifetime. Once her jarring shriek subsided, silence fell in what a few seconds before was a cacophony of commotion. Even Jon was quiet as he figured something was not quite right.

The woman was not only angry, she was embarrassed and more than a little sore. Susan was mortified. If looks could kill, my wife and son would have perished that day.

Susan mumbled a few words, then quickly picked up the kid and beat a hasty retreat to the car. From that day on, Jon had no shirts or pants with the Mill's label on them; his clothes were purchased in the safety of the mall. Not as inexpensive to the pocketbook, but a whole lot easier on the mind. Susan seldom went back to the store, probably in the fear she would run into a woman with a large, scarred backside.

• • •

This was too much for Avery and Kate, two young girls who had already gotten into their fair share of mischief. They started giggling, then laughing, looked at Susan, then started giggling again. "He really didn't do that, did he?"

• • •

Footprints at Big Star

Not only were we not particularly welcome at a textile mill, Jon also got us removed from the grocery store.

The Big Star was a few miles from home. Compared to today's sleek supermarkets, Big Star was a little frumpy and always in need of some maintenance. It was not a well-known chain or even a particularly large store, but it stocked the basics, and items on the weekly shopping list were easy enough to find. A major plus was that it was open until ten o'clock in the evening.

Perhaps because so few people shopped at that time, the store manager decided that replacing the floor tiles at nine o'clock would be a good idea. He must have reasoned that roping off a small area every night would not greatly inconvenience shoppers, and the entire job would be done in a few evenings. I am sure all was going splendidly until Susan realized that she needed to go to Big Star for a few items. Since I was doing homework with the girls, she took Jon with her.

Goo and mess were the furthest things from Susan's mind when they entered the store. They wheeled the cart from aisle to aisle and were making short work of the list. Jon was not always at her side, but Susan kept her eye out for his wandering tendencies. They were almost finished when she saw the roped-off area ahead. She took Jon's hand and without comment bypassed that area for her last few items. She should have retreated.

Jon was at the age when Star Wars cereals and other equally disgusting sweetened rubbish paraded as breakfast food. He loved to look at each box on the shelves and fantasize about its contents. Generally, he would stay put, transformed into Luke Skywalker or C-3PO for at least five minutes. However, while Susan was squeezing rolls of tissue to see if one was truly softer than the other, Big Jon decided to investigate the inviting ropes behind which the sticky and tacky tile adhesive had recently been applied. The cords and signage left no doubt that people were not supposed to go through there. However, he was so intrigued by the glistening goo, he simply stepped under the ropes to check it out a little closer. When Susan first heard the commotion, she had a sinking feeling that it happened once again—her son was on the loose.

The workmen were not in the store at that hour, but the manager had already been called upon to do something about this kid in the goo. Big Jon, clad in his Luke Skywalker sneakers, was inside the ring of ropes while outside the ring amused people started to gather, gawking and smiling at a small boy's pleasure of a new discovery. The manager, however, was not amused. The area was just wide enough that he could not reach Jon from outside the barrier, and the kid liked the place so much, he would always move just out of reach of the manager's outstretched arms.

By this time, a good-sized crowd had gathered and people were trying to coax Jon into coming out. Susan was also there, but she was whispering so that no one would know she was the mother. Nobody was going to go in after him and ruin a good pair of shoes. I can only assume the manager decided that this rubbernecking crowd was not buying any groceries and this kid was bad for not just the floor but for business. He plunged through the ropes and tried to tiptoe through the black tar in what were obviously very new, very shiny, and very expensive shoes. He stopped tiptoeing after the second failed effort to catch the kid, who by now, was enjoying all the excitement and attention. He finally caught him and hauled him out by the armpits, bellowing, "Whose child is this?"

Although she was trying to slip through the cracks in the floor, Susan had no choice but to claim him. The manager had every right to be angry, after all, he had completely and unquestionably ruined a two-hundred-dollar pair of shoes retrieving this kid, to say nothing of the entertainment he was providing. All in all, it was obvious that both the floor and the shoes would have to be replaced at considerable expense, so his sense of humor was not finely tuned as he turned Big Jon over to

his mother. I wasn't surprised when Susan ended this tale by telling me that she and Jon were no longer valued customers at Big Star.

There are some nice new tiles at Big Star now; I hope Susan and Jon see them before they need replacing again. We still have Jon's tar-studded shoes somewhere in the garage, and every time we start to throw them out, we smile and set them down again. I wonder if the manager still has his.

• • •

Jonathan and Mandy have a five-year-old of their own now. Avery is every bit as curious and energetic as her father and aunts. Every day they send us photos and comments of her antics. At home, she has an entire floor for her playhouse and her princesses, and with her imagination she often goes off to a world of her own. When they visited one cold evening last winter, we decided to mix up some hot chocolate. When I first took in the scent of that brew, I couldn't help myself. I looked at my granddaughter and asked, "Avery, did your dad ever tell you about how he made our whole house smell like a chocolate factory?" Both Mandy and Avery began to listen.

• • •

Road Work

Weather is fickle everywhere, but once we got the hang of the North Georgia seasons, we were reasonably weather-content. However, every now and then, we would have prolonged rain. In the early 1970s, Brook Benton, Ray Charles, and others popularized the song *Rainy Night in Georgia*, but they forgot to mention that along with those nights came rainy days as well.

We were in the midst of a three-day Georgia rain when I called home. Susan dutifully reported all quiet on the home front and that she was finally able to work on a few sewing projects she had been putting off. This was the calm before the storm.

Perhaps the dull weather also dulled the early warning system she had so finely developed with Laura and keenly honed with Heather. When I called again, her message was anything but calm; it was obvious she was not at all pleased. "I have been cleaning up after YOUR son," and then added somewhat snidely, "By the way, don't worry about the smell when you get home." When

I arrived home that evening, I was greeted with a weary wife and a not unpleasant fragrance. With a smile I said, "Have you and Jon been camping?" Oh my, not at all the correct greeting!

It turned out Jon wanted to play outside, but stuck in the house, playing with a few toy cars and trucks held his attention only until he could figure out something else. He was becoming more bored by the minute.

A month or so before this, we had built a very "rustic" sandbox outside. It was visited more by neighborhood cats than by neighborhood boys, but Jon must have remembered it that day. When Susan was busy upstairs, he simply decided to make his own sandbox on the kitchen floor. Rummaging around kitchen cabinets, he discovered the basic ingredients for his new creation: Nestlé chocolate powder and Four Star granulated white sugar. With the chocolate providing color and the sugar for consistency, he had the makings of a wonderful landscape.

It may not have been so bad had he not tried to construct the interstate highway system. He had roads running this way and that, and on those roads, his vehicles careened and banged into each other. Where no roads existed, tire tracks of sweetened chocolate powder crisscrossed one another. He had invented a video game without the video. His parents may have actually been pleased with his demonstration of being able to entertain himself, and we certainly could not fault his imagination.

That was before the addition of the water which allowed for expansion to about half the area of the kitchen floor, while the white rug just outside the kitchen was a perfect parking lot. Imagination is delightful, but when the kitchen becomes the motocross capital of the free world, we would have been hard-pressed to recognize the talent of even Michelangelo.

His mother first suspected all was not quite right when the faint smell of chocolate reached her nostrils. To be honest, she did not equate the aroma with trouble, but something else was not quite right; the house was far too quiet. As she stole upon the fragrant mud and roads, to her great credit, she screamed only once. Sewing forgotten, she morphed into "Cleanser Woman!" and would have made Johnson & Johnson proud. As Jon watched, she quietly and efficiently gathered brooms, vacuums, and

other assorted equipment designed for the removal of brown and white interstate systems from kitchen floors and rugs. Jon had been playing quietly and was having a nice time, and he was quite upset with the removal of his creation. Susan had to be equally creative to prevent another Thomas Textiles scene, so she did what all parents do in times of crisis. She bribed him.

There were few things our son treasured above all other, but George Lucas be praised, Star Wars was one of them. To many parents, Star Wars figures were one of the greatest tools of coercion ever invented for young boys. After fruitless negotiation, she secured his assistance with the promise of a new one. The fact that he had a rather large collection tells something about the number of his adventures.

When I arrived home that evening, I was greeted by an excited boy with Darth Vader in tow, an exhausted wife, and a strong smell of cocoa. Within a day or two, the smell had faded, the rug was almost white, and the floor was no longer tacky. Jon was off to yet-to-be-discovered adventures, and Susan had yet another story with which to entertain her friends. That evening, we picked up Darth where he lay by the table and quietly stole into Jon's room and placed him alongside Luke and Leia.

Even today, as we enjoy a cup of hot chocolate, it is hard not to laugh as we think of a busy little boy coated with chocolate and sugar doing what he did best—being a boy.

• • •

Throughout the story, Avery just kept smiling and laughing, interrupting with "Oh, no!" and "Daddy, you really did that?"

Later, when Mandy and daughter went to the pantry to get a few pretzels and nuts, you could see Avery's eyes widen and brain cogs whirling when she spied the cocoa container behind the trail mix. Mandy looked down and whispered, "Don't even think about it!"

• • •

Bathroom Decoration

The kids and grandkids were coming over. Even though it was "only" family, Susan put me to work cleaning up my office, vacuuming, and of course cleaning the bathrooms. On my hands and knees, with brush in one hand and Lysol cleanser in the other, I was making progress. I inadvertently hit the small table lamp on the bureau with my elbow, and it went crashing down. Susan rushed in to find me staring at the lamp, and smiling broadly. "What is the matter—why are you grinning?" she asked. I had to sit for a bit, and then said, "Do you remember Jon's adventures in the bathroom?" Susan sat down and could not help smiling as well. "Oh my, I had forgotten, but perhaps these are not stories that you should share with Avery."

Perhaps stories of children learning proper bathroom etiquette do not belong on the printed page, but Jon kept us laughing even about this. Most of the things that made his parents chuckle were "gross" to the girls at the time, and long forgotten. But after the Lysol was put away and the lamp picked up, we found ourselves drinking tea on the back deck, reminiscing once again.

At an early age, Jon was a child of habit. He did not have a lot of habits nor did they persist more than a few months, but they were very important to him. Where they came from, no one knew, and just as we were getting used to them, they disappeared.

Susan and I were a little concerned with some of his crazy behavior, but no more so than when we found him carrying two small reading lamps and a radio into the bathroom. Not just once, but on a routine basis. We looked at each other and shrugged our shoulders as confused parents do, but he was taking care of business and we were none the worse for his new lifestyle. But we were surely curious!

As he went inside, he switched off the overhead light. He then turned on one lamp, perched precariously by the sink, and then another that he had unceremoniously plunked into the dry sink itself. It was actually a rather pleasant atmosphere, as bathrooms go. Then the door closed. He would then place himself on the toilet and start to sing.

The singing, the noise from the radio, and the romantic lighting provided the backdrop for many of our son's forays into the wonderful world of toilet training. It was difficult to explain to our friends why lamps were in the sink and radios on the back of the bowl, but seeing Jon stealing down the stairs laden with electrical goods heading for the bathroom made any explanation worthwhile.

Nor did it take long for the next bathroom companion to join the other paraphernalia: the catalog. Jon loved catalogs. Their sections on toys, particularly Star Wars and G.I. Joe figures, spaceships, and airplanes, were a constant source of pleasure to him. Although he couldn't read, he identified every figure and vehicle ever pictured.

67

Here was a three-year-old boy, singing, listening to the radio, and reading the Sears catalog by dual reading lamps, at peace with nature. As complicated as this routine was, he simply would not function well until all his accoutrements were in place; then and only then would nature take its course. There was no sense in being in a hurry to go anywhere during this phase. Nothing, but nothing, could hurry this boy from his appointed rounds.

• • •

Avery listened with her mouth open. At four years old, she was absolutely aghast at her father's antics. Mandy did not know whether she should laugh out loud or just feel sorry for his parents. Thank goodness, Heather's kids were not there that day, or they would have thought it was the most hilarious thing they had ever heard.

Laura hardly cracked a smile. "What's wrong, Laura? I didn't mean to embarrass you; it was Jon, not you, doing all the entertaining." She looked at us and said, "It wasn't entertaining to me at the doctor's office!" Even Jon didn't know what she was talking about, but Avery wanted to hear more.

• • •

Behind Closed Doors

One of the more unpleasant tasks in parents' life is teaching the proper use of toilet paper. Even when very young, the girls were always discreet about such a topic. Not Jon. When he had finished nature's call, he would let his sisters know that they were needed. It did not matter if guests were present or not, Jon simply made his wishes known. The girls almost choked when their friends were over and Jon had taken up residence in the bathroom. Laura's good friends, Julie and Katie, first would look at Laura, listen again to the singing and other noises coming from behind closed doors, and burst into laughter. Laura did not share their humor, particularly after the day we visited the allergist.

If you ask an allergist, you would believe that Athens, Georgia is the seasonal allergy capital of the world. Their motto is "Either you have allergies or you will have them soon." I have always suffered, and the spectacular flowers of a Georgia spring made things worse. Even Laura was sneezing more than usual. When I went to the allergist for a battery of tests, it turns out I was lucky to be alive. He recommended shots for Laura and me, so we went for the needle twice a week.

Every now and then we would bring Jon along. The office was always bursting with men, women, and children who endured this archaic torture of "modern day" medicine. Jon was becoming bored as we awaited our turns to be punctured, and suddenly announced that he had to go to the washroom. The bathroom was right off the waiting room. Laura, knowing full well of Jon's joy of singing and noise making, was frantically trying to talk him out of this exercise. Not a chance!

He had made up his mind. Picking up a colorful book of bible stories found only in doctors' offices, he shut the door behind himself. About 30 seconds later, my name was called and I had to leave Laura in the waiting room with Jon just getting warmed up. Laura, starting to panic, silently begged me to hurry back before Jonathan finished. Normally, the shots proceeded rapidly but, on this day, more people were there than usual. Jon had already attracted considerable attention with his singing and Laura was studying her math book harder than ever in a valiant but largely unsuccessful effort to ignore him. As I was returning down the hall, the unspeakable occurred. The command, "Laura, wipe my bottom," was clearly audible from one corner of the room to the next. Laura was dying a quick death from acute embarrassment and then, thank goodness, her name was called for shots. As she sped by me, she hissed, "Dad, get your kid." I nonchalantly walked through the crowded room and opened the door just as the command was about to be repeated. When he saw me, he put the bible stories down,

completely oblivious to the human wreckage called Laura in the next room. Laura wouldn't sit with us when she returned, and from that day on, refused to go anywhere with Jon where there might be a bathroom.

• • •

By the time I had related the story, Jonathan had fled the room, Laura was still embarrassed, and Mandy and Avery, well, they were simply grinning from ear to ear. Laura apologized to her brother for even bringing it up, but said that she remembered those people staring at her as if it were yesterday. "That's the only time I ever remember looking forward to getting a needle!"

By then, Heather and family had joined us, and wanted to know what all the commotion was about. They had just returned from visiting their grandparents on David's side and stated how much they enjoyed visiting with them. I couldn't help but regret the fact that our kids had so seldom seen their grandparents and great-grandparents, especially Gorba. Heather looked up and somberly asked, "Dad, do you remember one of the last times we saw her? I will never forget."

· · ·

At Gorba's Place

My grandmother lived in Montreal, and had always affectionately been known as Gorba to her family. At the age of ninety-two, her body had slowed down considerably, but her mind was still sharp as a tack. She could out-debate anyone on almost any topic, including politics, world affairs, and health. She was also a wonderful storyteller and regaled her grandsons with stories of travel to exotic places. In short, she was extraordinary.

Unfortunately, age caught up with her and she decided that a nursing home was the best place to be. Her eyesight was failing and she kept in touch with the outside world mainly by means of her old Motorola radio, one of the few possessions she wanted to keep from her home, and at least as old as she was.

We did not get back to Montreal as often as I would have liked, but one summer we decided to make the long drive from Georgia. The three kids were packed in the car along with assorted and sundry baggage. We left in the middle of the night and drove and drove and drove. After two long days and longer nights during which we camped at places with names like Candyland and Zoopark, we finally arrived in Montreal. Everyone was exhausted, and in hindsight, we probably should have gone to see Gorba then as Jon would have fallen asleep without getting into mischief. But we waited until the next day.

Nursing homes, even the cheeriest and best run, are depressing places at best and horrific at worst. Regardless of the reasons they are there, most people go there to die, and they know it. Gorba lived on a floor populated mainly with elderly invalid women, many of whom also talked a fair amount in their sleep. They slept most of the day, and often sounded like they were having some very bad dreams. It was not a good fit for her, but she made the most of her time, making a few friends and doing her best to cheer them up. Most doors were open and except for the various noises coming from some of the rooms, the hall was quiet as a hospital. This is the scene that greeted us as we stepped off the second-floor elevator. It is amazing how even children stop their bickering when they arrive at such places.

It is a well-known fact that it takes only about fifteen minutes for a small boy to tire of hospital rooms. Gorba was sitting in her old chair from home and was delighted to hug Jonathan, whom she had never before seen. That was to be the last time Jon was quiet all afternoon. It started with the bed. Jon and his buddy, nine-year-old Heather, started bouncing on the bed. They weren't bouncing particularly vigorously but enough to be a nuisance to everyone else. He then discovered Gorba's cookies, a stash usually sufficient for a few weeks, offered some to Heather, and proceeded to attack the cookie tin without further delay. He was being a real pain. The result of the bouncing and eating was that Jonathan had to go to the bathroom. Gorba's vision may not have been 20/20 but there was nothing wrong with her hearing. The ensuing singing, other noises, and his final demands for help broke my grandmother's face into something that had been missing for a long time—a wonderfully wide smile. It beamed like a ray of sunshine into that room, and it simply took a normal little boy to break the clouds.

Heather asked if they could wander around the corridor a little. Few people were walking the halls, and we felt they could not get into too much mischief, to say nothing about wanting to be rid of them for a while. For almost fifteen minutes, the three of us enjoyed a calm, relaxing time, Laura catching her great-grandmother up with school and friends, and me reminiscing a little about old times. It was too good to last.

Jon and Heather burst wide-eyed and confused into the room. In their travels, they had come across some nurses, who, like most people in a nursing home, were delighted to see young, healthy children. They started babbling away to the kids but it sounded like a foreign language to them. In fact, it was. Montreal has been a bilingual city for years and more French was spoken in this facility than English. The nurses had been chattering in French while Heather and Jon just stared at them, wondering when they could run away. Once the nurses realized the problem, they quickly and effortlessly switched to English. This was our children's first insight into the necessity and benefits of a second language in today's complex world.

Continuing down the hall, they couldn't help but notice the many old people who had nothing to look forward to but the passage of time. Most were lying in their beds, some were watching television with vacant eyes, and others were mumbling in their sleep about more pleasant

times and places. I think these scenes unnerve adults more so than children, but Heather was uncomfortable and even Jonathan realized things were not right. They weren't frightened but were confused. They had gone to visit their great-grandmother but had experienced far more. They came face to face with the sounds and sights of loneliness and old age, and for the moment wanted to cover their ears and close their eyes. They learned a great deal about people that day even though their visit was short. They learned that although the body may become dull, the mind need not follow. Other visits to Gorba followed and while the children came to appreciate her a little better, the first visit was by far the most memorable.

A 60-Pound Lap Dog Named Patches

Recently, we were visiting Heather and her now teen-age children. The usual chaos was ensuing, and added to the mix were her two dogs, a rambunctious sort-of-Lab called Sadie, and a miniature poodle named Ella. I was oohing and cooing over Sadie while throwing Frisbees and kidding Ben by asking, "Can I take Sadie home?"

• • •

Ben and the others laughed, but then he asked, "Why don't you have a dog—did you ever have one?" I looked at him and said, "Didn't your mother tell you about Patches?"

• • •

We don't seem to be very good with animals. Perhaps it is genetic. I know many people who could not be without three cats, two dogs, a horse or two, and assorted fowl running around. They seem to be an extension of their personality, as if the genes for blue eyes may have been replaced by ones for pet ownership. Next time you meet a multiple pet person, check their eye color—few will have blue eyes.

Laura and Heather had both tried their hands with rabbits (they went to rabbit heaven within six months); gerbils (multiplied to twenty-eight gerbilettes, then given away to unsuspecting friends); fish (more often than not found floating belly-up); and even a duck (joined the rabbits). We put our feet down with caged birds—the sight of a parakeet or canary on its back with little feet in the air was too much to think about. The kids and Dad wanted a dog, but Susan is not a dog person, and the kids' history of animal care did not exactly beg another pet.

However, when Laura brought home the news that her friend's dog had delivered eight puppies, we were ripe for the picking. "Anna says they are a cross between a German shepherd and a Labrador retriever." These were the two breeds even Susan could tolerate, particularly the Labrador part. Many of our neighbors had dogs, most of which were reasonably well-behaved and harmless. Everyone we knew who had a Lab found them to be smart, obedient, and terrific around kids. Things were indeed looking up.

To Be In or Not to Be In

What joy one feels with a new puppy! They are cute furry balls of fluff with boundless energy and wet, loving tongues. Patches, so named because of light brown eye patches on his black German shepherd body, quickly became part of the family. However, we had a problem.

Normally, we would think of a dog as an indoor pet—that was simply the norm in northern climates. Since the kids and I had many allergies, none of which lessened in the South, we sought the advice of friends and neighbors. Our sneezing certainly came into our thinking, but then again, so did the fact that all our carpeting in the house was white (not a good idea in Georgia, regardless of dogs). As we quickly learned, while Georgia may be well known for peaches and peanuts, one of its lesser-known features is its red dirt. In North Georgia, loam or even brown soil is almost unheard of; the dirt is iron-ore rusty red clay. Based on these factors, we debated on whether Patches should be an inside or outside dog. By the fifth appearance of the carpet cleaner in the first couple of weeks, I started building an outdoor abode for Patches. The plan was to create a large pen, beneath a grove of handsome oak trees to provide shade. In the middle of this cramped playground would be a cozy dog house in which to thrive and grow.

Einstein He Was Not

Our puppy seemed to be growing in all the wrong places. His feet were huge to begin with and they just got bigger. Not only were his feet growing disproportionately large, his legs, like expandable stilts, kept getting longer and longer. Soon he looked like one of those crazy pickup trucks in which the chassis is jacked up about eight feet in the air. His small body floundered above those long legs and huge feet. He didn't walk, he loped, each leg going in a different direction and each foot flopping down wherever it happened to land. Running was out of the question as his legs were always at odds with each other.

The other puzzling thing was his brain. It didn't seem to function well, particularly for a Lab. Not that I knew much about dogs, but he seemed to be one of the dimmest I had come across. Slow to learn anything, and slower yet to respond, there appeared to be something missing. He was the only dog in his class to fail obedience school. Twice! However, his slowness certainly didn't extend to growing. He became significantly larger than we anticipated.

Weighing in at 60 pounds, he was the silliest-looking and seemingly most uncoordinated dog around. Within a year the body grew a little more in keeping with his legs, but nothing was in proportion to his feet; he was certainly not going to win any prizes at Westminster. Patches believed he was a toy poodle as he jumped on our laps and proceeded to snuggle and lick all parts of our crushed bodies. He never learned that while such lapping and licking were cute from a puppy, from a 60-pound adult they were rather painful. In fact, he didn't learn much. One day Susan threw her hands up in frustration and cried, "How can a dog that is half Labrador be incapable of even sitting?" Then Anna's mother, Carol, came over.

As she exited her car, Patches came loping up, legs everywhere, feet like stumps and tongue hanging out like Michael Jordan preparing for a monster dunk. Carol couldn't believe her eyes and she shouted, "It's Luke—I swear it's Luke!" It turned out that Luke was a rather large, rather dumb, and overly affectionate Irish setter; one look was all Carol needed to know that Luke was Patches' father. Suddenly, everything became clear. There was absolutely no Labrador retriever in this dog, from the top of his head down to his toenails. The appearance was German; the habits and disposition were Irish. What a combination!

Susan was distraught; she had always held out hope that the Lab in Patches would eventually surface. That was not going to happen. Irish setters are wonderful retrievers and hunters, featured in magazines like *Country Living* or *Garden & Gun*, but they are not particularly well suited to living in the inhumane confines of a small pen in a subdivision. His breed and disposition did not matter in the least to the children; he was their dog. Even with long legs, big feet, and a small brain, he was still Patches. But as he grew a little older, the need for wide open spaces came to the fore.

Escape From Alcatraz

One of the agreements to getting a dog was that Patches would be an "outdoor" dog and sleep outside, even though the children begged to have Patches in their beds with them at night. However, the kids reluctantly agreed and were happy to visit him outside and take him for walks throughout the neighborhood. Actually, in the way of parents everywhere, I ended up, quite happily, taking Patches for walks.

To my everlasting shame and guilt, Patches was relegated to an outdoor pen. I have been roundly criticized, scolded, and harangued about my lack of sensitivity in dog socialization. We thought we were building a little paradise for him, and that the new dog house with straw bedding would be a lovely dwelling for our much-loved dog. I placed shingles on the roof for waterproofing and a name tag over the door. With visions of Snoopy and Marmaduke in my head, I felt I had constructed a neat, tidy, and wonderful place to live. Too bad Patches did not agree. Attempting to reach his human family, he started to climb on the roof of the dog house, and every now and then reached up to eat the leaves and branches of the shade trees. Then one day, Patches decided that that this isolated life was not for him—it was time to make a break.

Digging proved to be the easiest way go. Numerous tunnels appeared under the fence, large enough to allow him to squeeze through. Not being highly gifted mentally, he would immediately romp to one of us, tail wagging, as if to say, "They couldn't keep me in, let's go play." I repaired each tunnel with rocks, large pieces of tree trunks destined for the fireplace, bricks left over from the builders, or anything heavy I could push up against the fence. Soon the beautiful pen took on the appearance of the Berlin Wall or the border crossing into Northern Ireland. Each time he was returned, he climbed on his roof to ponder future breakouts. Determination was his middle name.

He jumped out only once, when he thought he could clear the nearby fence from the roof of the dog house. As his front legs and upper body soared gracefully, his back legs and big hind paws tripped on the top. He landed unceremoniously at the base, tangled among fencing, bricks, and rocks. Shaking the detritus from his coat, he was soon happily on his way again. I was young and stupid, and Patches and I were locked in a battle of supremacy; we both believed we were the boss. After the third escape, I moved the dog house to the middle of the pen. He soon realized that soaring over the fence was no longer an option. Points to me!

Although the base of the pen looked like a bombed-out battlefield, entire trees were stripped of bark and leaves and yes, the dog house roof was quickly disintegrating, I believed Patches finally realized who was the alpha dog. To him this was obviously a game, and one he loved. His next efforts were quite unbelievable. Have you ever seen a dog climb a fence? Not jump, but climb?

As Patches started scaling the fence, one big paw over the other, the gauntlet was again thrown down. And he did it, time and time again. The challenge was on, man against beast. Like Wile E. Coyote, I would try anything to beat that roadrunner. And just like him, I would eventually admit defeat.

Bill was Carol's husband and Anna's father, and since he was partially responsible for this curious dog, he was consulted. "Why don't you try an electric fence?" was his suggestion. "It won't hurt him—he need only touch his nose to it once, and he will never try again." Patches, looking down from his dog house perch, heard me hum as I started working. Armed with wire, stakes, extension cord, and electric transformer, I was secure in my belief that man's technical superiority was no match for a dog. The kids were more than upset, figuring that I was trying to murder their beloved pet. I ran a wire near the top of the fence and plugged the contraption in. A red light blinked from the transformer with every pulse of electricity. I sat back on the deck waiting for the inevitable. Alcatraz was alive once more.

Patches began climbing the fence. I was anticipating, the kids were trembling, and Susan had long disappeared. When his snout hit the wire, he yelped and fell back, shaking his head vigorously. "It worked!" I shouted, although I was becoming much less pleased with my efforts as I noticed the tears of my children. I was not proud of the landscape before me, and I certainly did not plan on such Draconian efforts. However, once I assured the kids that such a small shock would not harm the dog, I was able to relax knowing that Patches and I had reached an agreement.

Such self-congratulation, however, was to be short-lived. I could not believe it when, not an hour later, he was ascending the heights once again. This time, touching the wire resulted in the same yelp, but the crazy dog continued anyway. Each hair on his body rose up in turn, from the tip of his nose through the entire length of his back. Yelping all the way, he made a final lunge to freedom, and, taking the wires with him, loped over to me as if to say, "Someone sure is trying to keep us apart." He planted one massive paw in my lap before he went off to find the kids. I was left sitting with a muddy paw print on my crotch, while I stared at torn pieces of useless wire in my hand. This battle had been lost.

There was no doubt I was being stubbornly stupid and reacting to egoist behavior rather than trying to solve the problem. If this was the Olympic event for stubborn, stupid animals, I would have taken home the gold medal. But I had not yet learned the meaning of humility. I was not done yet.

The final round of this battle had me banging stakes inside the pen, essentially creating a pen within the pen. Around the stakes, I strung two to three tiers of electric wire. I then repaired the wire on the top of the fence and set up a separate transformer. The once neat and tidy dog pen had been transformed into a gulag—all that was missing was barbed wire and guard towers. With the power on and red lights blinking like a pair of blood-shot cyclops, the combat resumed. Once again, children trembled, Dad anticipated, and Patches made his move.

He hit the inner wires and moved back with a jerk. Once again, he cautiously approached, once again was turned back. Did I dare hope this was working? Patches then backed up to the rear wire, started running, and

picking up speed, broke through those wires like a hot knife through warm butter. It was not painless, but certainly effective. I watched this bionic dog start climbing the fence again, and with the same noisy, hair-raising results as before, he broke free and ran about with joy. I knew then I was utterly defeated.

He, too, sensed my defeat and tried to cheer me up with his long, wet tongue. He was many things, one of them being a gracious winner. In the next few days, transformers, extension cords, wires, and dog pen were removed. The rocks, stumps, and bricks were picked up and the place once again resembled a residential landscape and not a concentration camp. Of course, the dog house, shingle-less by this time, and the pruned tree branches remained as a reminder of the Great Pen Escape.

Patches continued to lope, splatter us with his tongue and be loved by the children. Unfortunately, he was not as well loved in the neighborhood where he was making a nuisance of himself. His wanderlust and his resistance to staying in a pen were his eventual undoing. As much as we did love this crazy pet, eventually we all agreed, Carol and Bill included, that he would be far happier at Anna's house where he could romp and roam to his heart's content, and of course entertain many visits from the Armitage clan, particularly me, who still feels guilty every time I am nuzzled by our childrens' pets.

You Would Think . . .

You would think that having witnessed their father's stupidity, and the trauma of watching their pet turned into a lab rat, that the kids and Susan would never have a dog again. Not so.

Many years later, Laura had a puppy of her own. She was living in Colorado, and had rescued Hannah to live with her with roommates and their dogs. She took this lovely golden Lab everywhere, including the times she visited us in Athens. Each time she visited, the puppy was larger, but oh, how wonderful she was. After two years in Aspen, Laura accepted a new job in Atlanta and had to rent a small apartment, and it was soon apparent that Hannah could not stay cooped up in the apartment all day. When Laura asked us if Hannah could stay with us for a while, Susan and I did not hesitate. We had learned our lesson with Patches, and after a few months, there was no way we were returning her to Laura. Hannah became our constant companion in the house and out, and when she passed away twelve years later, we had lost a member of the family.

It turned out that all the kids had wonderful thoughts of Patches, their father's stupidity aside. Not only Laura, but throughout the years, Heather and Jonathan would not be without a dog in their lives.

So, thank you, Patches, for the memories.

WEDDINGS

"A daughter's your daughter for the rest of your life;
A son's a son 'til he takes a wife." S.E. Hall

Eventually, if all things go well, your kids grow up. If things go really well, they grow up healthy. If things go exceptionally well, they find a partner to share their lives. If things go unbelievably well, they remain happily married.

Stories about children and grandchildren can be incredibly boring to those not involved. However, for grandchildren, stories of their parents elicited smiles and occasional snorts of incredulity. They did not live the stories, but they were surely a product of them. But stories also emerge, out of the blue, as we get older, sit around with a glass of wine, and reminisce with friends. We chat about health and books we've read, and often complain about the kids and grandkids not calling. And oh, do we laugh together when the subject of daughters' weddings come up. The wine sure helps.

A Small Gathering

When Laura told us about Ray's proposal, we could not have been happier. We had heard many stories of wedding bedlam from our friends. We had attended weddings with hundreds of guests, incredible cuisine, flowing alcohol, and without doubt, thousands upon thousands of dollars being spent. This was not an option for either Laura or her parents. We agreed on a relatively small gathering of friends and family to reduce costs and anxiety. Not to say we did not face the wedding day with some fear and trepidation, but we had a plan and more importantly a budget. Ignorance is bliss.

Laura's problems with her wedding dress and veil almost took us over the top, because by that time, we believed we had resolved most of the other matters. Who knew that issues of bridegrooms, flowers, wedding venue, music, food, and drink would result in possible penury, not to mention astonishing levels of stress? However, the day was lovely, the Canadian family met the family from Macon, Georgia, and Susan and I sat back and absorbed the occasion. Our little girl was entering a new phase of life, one she and Ray were ready for, with Mom and Dad smiling through our tears. Other than a few of Laura and Ray's friends drinking too much, the ceremony and all the preparations fell into place. It was right out of Cinderella. In May of 2021, they celebrated their twenty-second anniversary.

Heather's nuptials were not quite as smooth.

Blue Lights in The Rain

To say that we were jubilant when Heather told us that someone wanted to marry her may be a bit of an overstatement—but not too much. As marvelous as Heather was, she still had a few rough edges, and she may not have been the easiest person to fall in love with. So when

David proposed, Susan and I were ecstatic. When Heather told us his parents were coming from Augusta to visit, we were more than a little nervous. We did not want to do anything to mess this up.

Somehow, we managed to pass muster and the wedding planning began. Good grief, we had done one already, how difficult could it be? Well, let me count the ways. Her brother, now playing college baseball at the University of Georgia, was not sure he could make the wedding because an important game had been rescheduled for that time. Heather had a point when she tersely asked, "If you had a baseball game, would you not come to my funeral either?" Little did she know that Jon begged and cajoled his coach into letting him leave the game early, and he arrived only slightly late. The weather was a little threatening, and unlike at Laura's wedding, we decided to rent a tent for the outdoor reception.

It poured rain.

Dress hems were soaked, dyed shoes ran, puddles puddled and it was unseasonably chilly. The rain finally slowed a little around ten that night and people were dancing, warmed by the wine, the camaraderie, and the band. Laura was so happy for her sister that we thought her face might forever freeze in a smile.

Heather was married!

Even the various other things that did not quite go according to plan were no longer bothering anyone—we thought we had it licked.

Then, about ten-thirty, blue police lights lit up the tent.

Who knew that there was a ten o'clock noise curfew? Not this wedding planner, that is for sure. Some of the neighbors had complained, and a policeman and his partner had arrived to close us down. As a dad, I already knew that a "Hollywood fairy tale" wedding was not to be, but getting your daughter's wedding shut down by the law was not something I wanted Heather to have to recall to her future family.

I rushed out of the tent, introduced myself and tried to appeal to their better senses. I inquired if they were fathers, and begged them to allow us to continue a little longer. We would turn down the volume, we would be less boisterous—in essence, wasn't there some way we could keep this going for another hour or so? Distracted by the noise and lights in the tent, Heather was oblivious to this little drama outside. She was the last person I needed in the middle of this.

The officers were polite and pleasant enough, but I could tell I was losing the argument; they were getting tired of me. I wondered how I was going to break this news to my daughter. As I resigned myself to this chore, I looked up through the falling mist to see Heather's siblings approaching. Wet and bedraggled, they pleaded for just a little more time for their sister's big night. They asked politely but with obvious feeling, for just one more hour. The officers looked at the kids, then at each other, and with a smile, started to turn away. With that, they asked us to keep the music down, try to reduce the noise, and make sure guests were gone by eleven-thirty. Laura and Jon thanked the men and immediately went back to the party.

Heather and her mother never knew.

In May of 2021, Heather and David celebrated their 19th anniversary.

TRADITIONS

Like parents everywhere, there have been many times when we wondered if any of our traditions would be carried on by the kids as they grew up. It seems parents just assume that at least bits of their heritage would be wholly embraced and carried on by their children.

What Are You Doing Here?

We tried to visit family in Canada when the kids were young, even to the point of carrying them from their beds at 4:00 in the morning, loading them in the trusty old station wagon, and making the long drive home. We felt it was important for them to appreciate their roots. Perhaps going at Christmas time was not a good idea as it was always cold and blizzarding when we made the treks from one family household to another. When they complained, I explained that it was only weather, and people who lived here actually enjoyed it.

They still remember one New Year's Eve in Ontario. It was windy, bitterly cold, and snowing as we drove from somewhere to somewhere else. The kids were shivering in the back when we were stopped for a routine sobriety test. As I answered the questions, including where we were from, the officer noticed the quivering mass in the back. He stuck his head through the window and said, "You're from Athens, Georgia?" As they nodded yes, he then blew a hole in my efforts to keep my children

Canadian by asking, quite incredulously, "What are you doing here!?" Winter travels to the homeland became even less frequent.

Torture Pie

One of the traditions Susan and I really loved was incorporating some French-Canadian cuisine, especially at Christmas. French onion soup with cheese overflowing, crisp warm French baguettes, and my favorite— tourtière. Tourtière is a traditional meat pie, combining minced pork, onions, spices, and herbs, baked in a conventional piecrust. Susan's recipe was better every year and we all looked forward to the aroma, the taste, and the tradition. Or at least I thought we did.

As Ray and Laura's relationship became more serious, she would invite him to the house around Christmas. Since he was a special guest, I offered him some tourtière and reveled in the knowledge that I was doing my part to cement this relationship. As a boyfriend, then as a fiancé, and then as a newly married young man, he was a perfect gentleman, saying *yes sir* and *no sir* at the correct times.

The next Christmas, Ray, Laura, Heather, and Jon were home when Laura took me aside. "Dad, can we not serve tourtière this year? Ray does not really like it." I could not believe my ears—who could possibly not love this recipe? "Well," she replied, "He asked if we had to have torture pie again." Once the word got out, all the kids thanked Ray profusely. They too were only putting on a façade; they had always thought of it as torture pie as well. One more tradition shot, but then again, all the more for me!

Christmas Morning

When Susan got off the phone with Heather recently, and filled me in on Heather's incredibly chaotic lifestyle, we once again asked ourselves if these were really our children. We were not doing too well in the tradition department: less appreciation for the homeland, no gratitude for traditional gastronomy, and many other ways in which the kids expressed themselves in the home and the raising of the grandkids. However, one of our traditions has continued.

We loved to extend Christmas Day for as long as possible. Like parents everywhere, we hid presents—like

kids everywhere, they hunted them down. We even told them if they got up too early on Christmas Day, buckets of water would fall from their doors. After they were in bed on Christmas Eve, we would fill the stockings, and then cover "Santa's presents" with towels so they would not see them when they came down to the tree. To extend Christmas, we had the kids join us in bed while they dumped their stockings, and then went down again to enjoy an "egg bake," another Canadian tradition. They could hardly stand themselves, excitedly glancing at the wrapped presents and especially anticipating what was under the towels. We took so long doing presents that by the time family from Canada or their friends would be calling to share their day, we were still eating egg bake. Susan and I loved the towels, the sharing of stockings, and the prolonged excitement, but realized when the kids left the house, such silliness would not likely continue.

Yet, on every Christmas morning at all three houses, Santa's gifts are under wraps. Breakfast is served after stockings, and the excitement of Christmas is prolonged for the grandchildren. We can't help but smile as we share this lovely ritual—tradition is alive and well after all.

STORY MAKING MACHINES

As Laura, Heather, and Jonathan married and started families of their own, we were as proud as could be, but perhaps not without a little melancholy. Did we spend enough time with them, will they include us in their memories as often as we do in ours? As each sibling left the house, I also had to admit to being a little scared that perhaps we had peaked as parents. It was our time to watch from the sidelines as occasional cheerleaders, rather than full-time ones. It turns out that part is always simple; they are still very easy to cheer for.

There is really no way to finish a story book like this. Stories, by their very definition, are living things, perhaps embellished by the storyteller, and always bring characters to life. Every parent could write a book like this, because every child is a story-making machine. Most of us are content to allow stories to wash over us, to enjoy them, and to move on. While we may not put pen to paper, we are ever caught up in the passage of time. When friends get together, invariably the subject of children and grandchildren comes up, and heads nod in agreement when a comment about how fast they grow is uttered, or how kids today just don't seem to have the same appreciation for the things we did.

However, we stand back, we get out of their way, and hope that we did as well as we could with our time together. We even hope, perhaps naively, that our children will take our approaches to parenting and evolve into better versions of ourselves. Good luck with that! There isn't a week that goes by that we don't wonder aloud if they are really our children. We look at each other, we question their parenting, and again wonder aloud if we taught them anything. Then we realize they are being exactly like us, and making stories of their own. Maybe they too will write them down.

EPILOGUE: WE ALL SURVIVED

Laura

Despite the wedding dress fiasco, or maybe because of it, Laura and Ray have been married for twenty-three years. Laura quietly overcame her fear of the world and is grateful for the empathy she learned growing up as the tall, shy kid. She is the supervisor of the Speech Language Pathology department in a large hospital in Macon, Georgia. Mary Grace is a sophomore at the University of Georgia, and Hampton is a junior in high school. They still love hearing stories about their mom.

Heather

Heather and David live in Augusta, Georgia. Drew is a senior in high school, the twins Will and Ben are freshmen in high school, and Kate is about to join them there. Although they continue to keep their mother occupied, her independence has not diminished over the years. Heather coordinates outpatient diabetic education at a hospital in Augusta, and has started her own company to educate the community about diabetes. Heather's feistiness and strong will have been passed down to her children, who continue to make stories they will share with their children. The twins no longer accompany her to the car wash.

Jonathan

As the youngest, Jon was a wonderful plaything for his sisters, who dressed him up at every opportunity. He found his passion in athletics, excelling in all sports and playing baseball in the San Francisco Giants organization. He uses his other passion, mathematics, to work as a data scientist in Indianapolis, Indiana. He and Mandy have been married for seven years and are busily recording stories of the adventures of their five-year-old daughter Avery.

Mom and Dad

They continue to be active in lovely Athens, Georgia. Allan has become a successful horticulturist while his very patient wife spent her career helping others as a nutritionist, nurse, and eventually as head of an occupational health facility. They celebrate the fact that their children are still very close and talk with each other every week. Mostly, they shake their heads in disbelief at their good fortune, and enjoy hearing from their children about the antics of their grandchildren.

Mom and Dad, Heather, Jonathan and Laura, then

Standing: Jonathan, Allan, Susan, Drew
Sitting: Laura, Hampton, Mary Grace, Will, Ben, Heather, Kate, 2009

Heather, Jonathan and Laura, then

Heather, Jonathan and Laura, 2020

Laura and family, 2020

Heather and family, 2020

Jonathan and family, 2021

The indomitable Patches

Back: Susan, Mary Grace, Laura, Allan, David, Drew, Heather
Front: Ben, Kate, Will, 2020

About the Author and Illustrator

Allan Armitage spends most of his time watching the plants flower and the grass grow. He plays pickleball with his wife, strums a little guitar, plays some tennis and tells stories. In his real life, he is a well-known horticulturist, author, speaker and the recipient of numerous awards for writing and contributions to the world of plants, flowers and gardening.

All in all, he sounds pretty boring.

However, he is never boring when he is telling stories, particularly about the adventures and calamities of his young family as they were growing up. In this delightful book, Allan shares stories that make us all smile, because as he is the first to admit, anyone could write a book like this. The only difference is that he wrote them down as they unfolded, over forty years ago.

Anyone who reads even one of the tales will not be able to suppress the memory that a similar thing happened with their children. Some stories will strain credibility, but most will result in a long amusing smile, while others may actually result in rather impolite belly laughs.

This is a story book about all our children, grandchildren, nieces and nephews, because as Allan says, "Children are Story Machines," and there is nothing boring about any of them.

Valarie Nichols is an award winning Graphic Designer and freelance Illustrator, living and working from her home in Tucker, Georgia. Through illustration and design of Annual Reports, Valarie was the recipient of the Gold Award from Creativity 27: The Best Advertising and Design from 40 Countries Around the World, and the Top Five Award from Ragan Communications for Annual Report design. Through her devotion to volunteerism in the community, Valarie is a founding member of Community Art Tucker and designed, orga-

nized, and headed up a public art installment of a mural on the Tucker Recreation Center in 2015. She has designed and installed many murals for clients throughout the Atlanta area, and as a Master Gardener and beekeeper, Valarie also uses her design skills in creating landscape designs for clients in the Atlanta Metro area. "Creativity is contagious, pass it on" —Albert Einstein

Other Titles by Allan M. Armitage

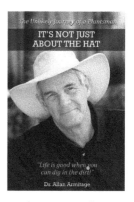

Of Naked Ladies and Forget-Me-Nots
The Stories Behind the Names of Some of Our Favorite Plants

Legends in the Garden
Who in the World Is Nellie Stevens?
with Linda L. Copeland

It's Not Just About the Hat
The Unlikely Journey of a Plantsman

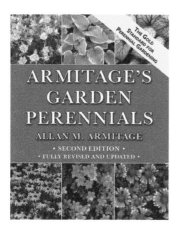

Armitage's Garden Perennials
Second Edition

Herbaceous Perennial Plants
A Treatise on Their Identification, Culture, and Garden Attributes
Fourth edition

all books are available at www.allanarmitage.net/shop